CAMPAIGN 283

# COWPENS 1781

Turning point of the American Revolution

**ED GILBERT & CATHERINE GILBERT**

ILLUSTRATED BY
GRAHAM TURNER
*Series editor Marcus Cowper*

First published in Great Britain in 2016 by Osprey Publishing,
PO Box 883, Oxford, OX1 9PL, UK
1385 Broadway, 5th Floor, New York, NY 10018, USA

E-mail: info@ospreypublishing.com
Osprey Publishing, part of Bloomsbury Publishing Plc
© 2016 Osprey Publishing Ltd

A CIP catalog record for this book is available from the British Library.

ISBN: 978 1 4728 0746 5
PDF e-book ISBN: 978 1 4728 2238 3
e-Pub ISBN: 978 1 4728 2237 6

Editorial by Ilios Publishing Ltd, Oxford, UK (www.iliospublishing.com)
Index by Marie-Pierre Evans
Typeset in Myriad Pro and Sabon
Maps by Bounford.com
3D bird's-eye views by The Black Spot
Battlescene illustrations by Graham Turner
Originated by PDQ Media, Bungay, UK
Printed in China through World Print Ltd.

16 17 18 19 20   10 9 8 7 6 5 4 3 2 1

## ARTIST'S NOTE

Readers may care to note that the original paintings from which the colour
plates in this book were prepared are available for private sale. The
Publishers retain all reproduction copyright whatsoever. All enquiries
should be addressed to:
Graham Turner, PO Box 568, Aylesbury, Buckinghamshire, HP17 8ZX
www.studio88.co.uk
The Publishers regret that they can enter into no correspondence upon this
matter.

## ACKNOWLEDGMENTS

Cowpens has been extensively studied and written about, often with
contradictory conclusions. Our analysis is based on period records –
particularly depositions given for Federal Pension Applications – and
personal inspection of the battlefield. The exhaustive work of Will Graves
(http://revwarapps.org/) and Bobby Gilmer Moss (author of *The Patriots at
the Cowpens*) served as finder's guides to individual Federal Pension
Applications. Resources were provided by the National Archives and
Records Administration, the British National Archives, Library of Congress,
Daughters of the American Revolution archives, Fondren Library (Rice
University), The University of Houston Library, The Clayton Center for
Genealogical Research (Houston Public Library), The Anne S. K. Brown
Collection (Brown University Library), the US Marine Corps History Division,
and the National Park Service. Elizabeth Gilbert-Hillier researched
Cornwallis' original correspondence files, including previously unpublished
materials, in the British National Archives. The Katy branch of the Harris
County Library system provided interlibrary loan services. Local support
was provided by: Martin Mongiello (American Revolutionary War Living
History Center, Grover NC); Virginia Fowler, John Slaughter, and other staff
members (National Park Service, Cowpens National Battlefield); and re-
enactors and groups, particularly Ed Forte (New Jersey Light Infantry), Ed
Harrelson (3rd Continental Light Dragoons), and the New Acquisition
Militia.

## DEDICATION

For Lilly Catherine Gilbert.

## THE WOODLAND TRUST

Osprey Publishing are supporting the Woodland Trust, the UK's leading
woodland conservation charity, by funding the dedication of trees.

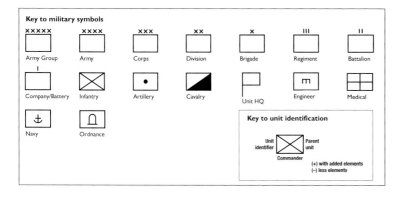

**Key to military symbols**

| | | | | | | |
|---|---|---|---|---|---|---|
| ✕✕✕✕✕ | ✕✕✕✕ | ✕✕✕ | ✕✕ | ✕ | III | II |
| Army Group | Army | Corps | Division | Brigade | Regiment | Battalion |
| I | ⊠ | ⊡ | ◤ | ⚑ | ⊓ | ⊞ |
| Company/Battery | Infantry | Artillery | Cavalry | Unit HQ | Engineer | Medical |
| ⚓ | ⊓ | | | | | |
| Navy | Ordnance | | | | | |

**Key to unit identification**

Unit identifier — Parent unit

Commander

(+) with added elements
(−) less elements

# CONTENTS

# Strategic situation North America, December 1780–January 1781.

QUEBEC

Lake Superior

Lake Huron

Lake Michigan

Lake Ontario

Lake Erie

QUEBEC

MASSACHUSETTS

NEW HAMPSHIRE

NEW YORK

MASS. ● Boston

PENNSYLVANIA

RHODE ISLAND
CONNECTICUT

New York

Philadelphia

NEW JERSEY

Baltimore ●

DELAWARE

MARYLAND

SPANISH TERR.

INDIAN RESERVE

Ohio River

VIRGINIA

Mississippi River

NORTH CAROLINA

SOUTH CAROLINA

GEORGIA

Charlestown

WEST FLORIDA

Savannah

St. Augustine

ATLANTIC OCEAN

EAST FLORIDA

Gulf of Mexico

N

American controlled
British controlled
Tribally controlled (British allies)
Contested
Lead mines

0       250 miles
0     250km

# ORIGINS OF THE CAMPAIGN

I knew my adversary and was perfectly sure I should have nothing but downright fighting.
(Brigadier-General Daniel Morgan)

Cowpens was one of the decisive battles of American history, but has long been overshadowed by less decisive Revolutionary War battles. In part this resulted from the geographic isolation of the Southern Campaign from the seats of political power and memoirists. Most of the commanders were not of the politically influential classes of colonial society; the American commander, Daniel Morgan (one of the great generals of American history), was a self-educated frontiersman.

Still, 18th-century and early 19th-century historians and the leaders of the new republic widely acknowledged the significance of Cowpens. But when South Carolina became the first state to secede from the Union in 1861, history began to change. The Southern Campaign was almost entirely written out of mainstream American history. Today Cowpens figures little in the minds of most Americans except regional historians and military professionals.

To fully understand Cowpens it is necessary to grasp the long regional history that led up to the battle, the culture of the local militia that made up such a large – and ultimately decisive – part of the American force, and the culture and personalities of not only the generals but the ordinary fighting men on both sides.

The December 1774 Boston Tea Party triggered passage of the Coercive Acts, which abrogated the last vestiges of colonial self-rule. Rather than intimidating the rebels, the Acts hardened resistance. (Anne S. K. Brown Collection)

# THE WAR IN THE SOUTH

The origins of the colonial rebellion lay in the affluent coastal cities, primarily in New England. Merchants and townsfolk were those most impacted by the Townshend Acts that imposed taxes on staple commodities like tea, and heavy taxes on luxury goods and commercial raw materials like "wine, molasses [used to make rum], sirup, [decorative] paneles, coffee, sugar, pimiento, indigo, foreign paper, glass and painter's colours."

In the southern colonies the most affluent city by far was Charlestown in South Carolina, home of social and political elites grown fabulously wealthy from the export of rice and indigo. The "rice kings" held a tight grip on the colony's Commons House of Assembly, though 80 percent of the non-slave population lived in the interior, or "back country." The delegates to the Assembly grew increasingly resentful of the Crown Governor's authority on issues dealing with trade agreements since measures decided upon by the Assembly could be arbitrarily nullified by the Governor.

In contrast to the dominantly English and Church of England (Anglican) coastal communities, the back country was a patchwork of ethnic and religious communities: Germans, Swiss, Dutch, Welsh, French, and Scots-Irish, with Roman Catholics and an astonishing variety of Protestant sects. Numerically and culturally dominated by the largely Presbyterian, Baptist, or Methodist Scots-Irish, the back country settlers were scorned by the coastal elites, and effectively disenfranchised. Voting districts were not defined and polling places were located only along the coast.

Whig and Loyalist political tactics included beatings, tarring and feathering, symbolically pouring boiling tea down the throat, and sometimes lynching. (Library of Congress)

Most settlers despised the coastal elites more than distant Parliament. There were few courts or schools, and the primary duty of the seldom-seen sheriff was to collect taxes that funded the official Anglican Church. Under colonial law non-Anglican marriages had no legal standing; spouses were fornicators (punishable under law if someone in authority so decided), their children illegitimate. In the aftermath of the First Cherokee War (the local name for the French and Indian War of 1754–63, the North American theater of the global Seven Years War) the frontier grew increasingly lawless, plagued by outlaw gangs. This was of little consequence to the Governor or the Commons House; the settlers were useful only to hold the hostile Cherokee and Creek tribes at bay.

Resentment boiled over into the 1768–71 War of the Regulation, pitting organized vigilantes against the colonial government. Civil war was narrowly averted, and a few reforms were grudgingly instituted. In the 1770s the

The disasters in the Saratoga battles of 1777 triggered the British "Southern strategy." Artist E. C. Yohn accurately depicted written descriptions of Burgoyne's surrender. (Lodge)

fomenters of rebellion in Charlestown were dismayed by tepid support in the back country, but internal strife resulted in clashes between Loyalist and Whig (rebel) militia in the Snow Campaign of December 1775. (The rebels first called themselves Whigs, later Patriots, and eventually Americans.)

A botched British attack on Charlestown in June 1776 led to a period of Whig ascendancy. Outspoken Loyalists were subjected to violence by Whig hotheads: confiscation of property, beatings, tarring and feathering, torture, and exile. Many Loyalists took refuge in British-controlled East Florida, from whence they plagued Georgia. For two years the British left South Carolina, with its lucrative foreign trade that helped fund the rebellion, alone.

In London, exiles from the southern colonies had the ear of King George III and his advisors (primarily Lord George Germain), convincing them that Crown sentiment was strong in the south. Inexpensive British victories there would carve off the southern colonies, and isolate troublesome New England. Trying to hold together a global empire against French, Spanish, and Dutch competition, Britain was attempting to suppress the rebellion on the cheap. The stalemate with George Washington's elusive armies in the north, and disastrous British defeats at Saratoga in September and October of 1777, made a southern strategy attractive. Encouraged by the Saratoga battles, France recognized the new American government and in retaliation Britain declared war on France in March 1778. In June Spain entered the war against Britain.

In December 1778 a British army easily seized Savannah, Georgia, the first in a string of rebel disasters. American

Following the massacre of Patriots by Tarleton's Loyalist British Legion at The Waxhaws (May 29, 1780), "Tarleton's Quarter" became a Patriot rallying cry. (Unidentified artist, Anne S. K. Brown Collection)

At the battle of Camden (August 16, 1780) Horatio Gates' Patriot militia broke in the face of a British bayonet charge, and their flight fatally disrupted the ranks of Gates' Continentals. The defeat ended organized American resistance in the south, and triggered a horrific partisan war. (Pamela Patrick White, www.whitehistoricart.com)

countermeasures were hampered by having to move troops south by land to avoid the Royal Navy. A Franco-American siege failed to recapture Savannah in September and October 1779, and on May 12, 1780 ill-prepared Charlestown fell after a brief siege led by General Sir Henry Clinton. The surrender effectively eliminated the American Continental Army in the south.

American Continentals and militia units not captured in Charlestown retreated toward North Carolina. Other rebels accepted British paroles – freedom in exchange for promising never again to take up arms against the Crown.

Clinton was determined to crush the last vestiges of rebellion. He dispatched hard-charging Lieutenant-Colonel Banastre Tarleton and his Loyalist British Legion in pursuit of Continentals and rebel militiamen under Colonel Abraham Buford retreating toward North Carolina. On May 29 Tarleton overtook Buford at The Waxhaws. Outnumbered, Tarleton solicited surrender; Buford declined and attempted to retreat. When Tarleton's hardened veterans charged into the novice Americans, many threw down their arms in surrender. Tarleton's men slaughtered most of those who surrendered, mutilating the wounded. The Waxhaws incident was the first in a string of atrocities committed by the Legion, and precipitated a bitter partisan war. "Tarleton's Quarter" and "Buford's Play" became Patriot rallying cries that would have terrible implications.

On June 8 Clinton departed for New York, leaving General Charles Cornwallis in command of the Southern Army, and holding a tiger by the tail. Before departing Clinton issued a unilateral declaration that paroles applied only to those rebels captured within Charlestown proper. All others would have to swear a new oath of fealty, and promise to take up arms against their erstwhile comrades. This high-handed act enraged rebels who otherwise would have sat out the ensuing war.

# Significant actions in and near South Carolina.

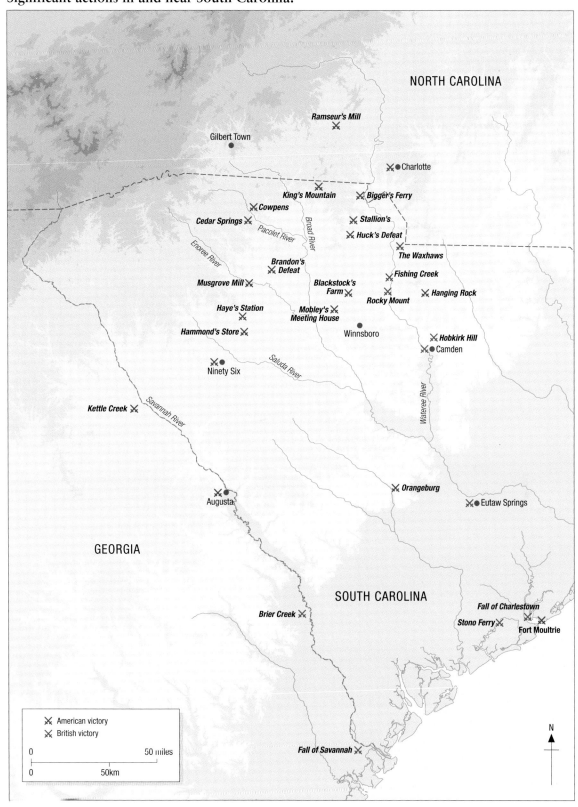

NORTH CAROLINA

Ramseur's Mill

Gilbert Town

Charlotte

King's Mountain

Bigger's Ferry

Cowpens

Cedar Springs

Stallion's

*Pacolet River*

*Broad River*

Huck's Defeat

*Enoree River*

Brandon's Defeat

The Waxhaws

Fishing Creek

Musgrove Mill

Blackstock's Farm

Rocky Mount

Hanging Rock

Haye's Station

Mobley's Meeting House

Winnsboro

Hammond's Store

*Saluda River*

Hobkirk Hill

Camden

Ninety Six

*Wateree River*

Kettle Creek

*Savannah River*

Orangeburg

Augusta

Eutaw Springs

GEORGIA

SOUTH CAROLINA

Fall of Charlestown

Brier Creek

Stono Ferry

Fort Moultrie

American victory
British victory

0          50 miles

0          50km

Fall of Savannah

N

9

Local Loyalists commenced a retaliatory reign of terror against the rebels, to which the British army turned a blind eye; at times the army participated in the looting, arson, rape and murder. Patriot leaders who had accepted parole had their homes looted and burned, others were summarily imprisoned. Predation on local families and Loyalist destruction of Presbyterian "sedition houses" outraged hitherto neutral colonists, and sent the colony spiraling further into civil war. Cornwallis largely abandoned the back country, establishing a string of fortified towns to screen the important port cities as the war grew in scope and savagery.

The Continental Congress dispatched another army led by the politically ambitious but tactically hapless General Horatio Gates. Gates had fumbled badly at Saratoga, with the day saved by his subordinates. Gates' usurpation of the credit for Saratoga and his continuing intrigues to replace George Washington as commander-in-chief drove talented leaders like Daniel Morgan and Benedict Arnold to resignation or treason.

Gates' army included some of the best Continental regiments, led by German-born Major-General Johann de Kalb. Driving his army through country barren of supplies, Gates was brutally defeated at Camden, South Carolina on August 16, 1780. Gates' untested militia stampeded in the face of British bayonets, disrupting and abandoning the Continentals. De Kalb was killed, and hundreds of Continentals disappeared into the British prison hulks anchored in Charlestown Harbor. Henry Wells of Delaware recorded that about half his regiment died in battle, from disease, and "hard treatment &c while prisoners. Two of my cousins fell into the hands of the enemy at Camden, one died from the severity of their treatment – the other lived to be exchanged, but he returned with a shattered constitution."

The rebel cause had reached its nadir. In brutal partisan warfare Loyalists wreaked revenge for past wrongs, and Whigs retaliated. But far from thousands of Loyalists rallying to the flag, British recruiting efforts faltered. In the northern and central colonies the stalemate continued. In late 1780 the Continental Congress sent another, far more competent, field commander south. The stage was set for the most decisive phase of the war.

Some captured Patriots enlisted in Loyalist units rather than face lingering death aboard prison hulks in Charlestown Harbor. As many as 40 percent of all Patriot deaths occurred while in British captivity. (Lossing)

# CHRONOLOGY

**1764–71**

In the back country resentment grows over unfair taxation, embezzlement by colonial officials, and lack of legislative representation and courts of law. The War of the Regulation pits vigilante groups against the colonial government.

**1775**

Rebels seize Crown ships and facilities. Georgia and South Carolina militia clash with British regulars. In December the Snow Campaign pits Patriot against Loyalist militias.

**1776**

**June 21–29** — A botched British attack fails to recapture Charlestown. Skirmishes between Patriot militia and British forces grow in number and intensity.

**January 1777–December 1778**

Britain concentrates on subduing New England.

**1778**

**December** — A British army lands to implement the Southern Strategy, and captures Savannah on December 29.

**1779**

**September 24–October 19** — A Franco-American force besieges Savannah. The repulse of the final, failed assault is the bloodiest day of the entire war.

**1780**

**April 1** — The British besiege Charlestown. Naval and land skirmishes occur through broad areas of the South.

**April 14** — Banastre Tarleton defeats an American force at Monck's Corner to emerge as one of the most ruthless and feared British leaders.

**May 12** — Charlestown falls.

**May 29** — Tarleton defeats Abraham Buford at The Waxhaws, South Carolina. Tarleton is acquitted of tolerating atrocities in an ensuing court martial.

**June 1–July 12** — Captain Christian Huck of Tarleton's Legion begins a reign of terror and murder, burning Presbyterian "sedition houses" and turning the war into the "Presbyterian Rebellion."

**August 16** — General Horatio Gates is decisively defeated at Camden, South Carolina. The war degenerates into a savage partisan conflict.

| | |
|---|---|
| September 26 | Cornwallis marches into North Carolina; the British Legion under temporary command of George Hanger suffers a minor defeat at Charlotte. |
| October 7 | Major Patrick Ferguson is trapped at King's Mountain, South Carolina, and most of Cornwallis' Loyalist militia are destroyed. |
| November 20 | Tarleton corners Sumter's militia and State troops at Blackstock's Plantation, South Carolina, but is decisively defeated. Three successive defeats and growing partisan activity in his rear force Cornwallis to break off his invasion of North Carolina. |
| December | Nathanael Greene assumes command of the battered American Southern Army in North Carolina. He divides the army, and marches into South Carolina. Raids by partisans and Morgan's light troops fuel Cornwallis' growing anxiety for the security of the base at Ninety Six. |

## 1781

| | |
|---|---|
| January 1–16 | Cornwallis orders Tarleton to break off pursuit of Francis Marion's low-country guerrillas to deal with Morgan. Tarleton aggressively pursues Morgan, but Cornwallis lingers behind, awaiting the arrival of reinforcements marching from Charlestown. |
| January 17 | Tarleton falls upon Morgan's force at Hannah's Cowpens, and is decisively defeated. About 1,000 of Cornwallis' best troops are lost. |
| January 18–February 14 | After a false start, Cornwallis pursues Morgan and Greene for some 200 miles (325km) toward Virginia over muddy and frozen roads. American forces escape across the rain-swollen Dan River into Virginia. |
| February 17–March 3 | Cornwallis rebuilds his army in Wilmington, North Carolina. |
| March 15 | Greene marches back south and confronts Cornwallis at Guilford Courthouse, North Carolina. Cornwallis wins a tactical victory, but his army is gutted. |
| April 5–June 5 | Greene's army returns to South Carolina, and with local partisans systematically reduces British posts. |
| April 25 | Cornwallis marches his battered army from Wilmington toward Virginia. |
| September 8 | Greene attacks the British at Eutaw Springs, South Carolina and suffers a tactical defeat, but the British have incurred irreplaceable losses. |
| October 19 | Besieged by American and French forces at Yorktown, Virginia, Cornwallis surrenders. |
| November 18–December 17, 1782 | The British evacuate bases at Wilmington, Savannah, and Charlestown. The Patriot militias turn to subduing the British-allied Cherokee. |

## 1783

| | |
|---|---|
| December | The Treaty of Paris formally ends the war. |

# OPPOSING COMMANDERS

The commanding officers at Cowpens came from starkly different cultures. British officers were largely the sons of wealthy families who purchased military commissions that allowed them to rise financially, socially, and politically. Competence was not so important as reckless bravery, or the willingness to expend the lives of common soldiers. In training and experience they were the beneficiaries of centuries of European dynastic warfare. Much of that experience was not applicable in warfare as practiced in North America, but experience in the French and Indian War had taught the British Army many lessons about frontier warfare.

The commanders of the rebel forces were self-taught soldiers, veterans of warfare with the Cherokee and Creek tribes. They were mostly descendants of lesser members of English and Scots-Irish society who had immigrated to the colonies to escape the society that elevated their opponents to positions of wealth and power. While the meddling of the Continental Congress was a constant problem for Commander-in-Chief George Washington, military disasters in the South finally forced Congress to allow Washington to choose his own officers for this critical campaign. He chose extraordinarily well.

Clinton's departure left General Charles Cornwallis to attempt control of a rebellious population. An able administrator, Cornwallis' downfall was due in part to his misplaced trust in subordinates. (NARA)

## BRITISH

Born into an aristocratic family, **General Charles Cornwallis** was educated at Eton and Cambridge, entered the army at 19, and served in the Seven Years War. An able administrator and one of the brightest British commanders, he fought in the northern colonies, but returned to England when his wife fell fatally ill. Requesting reassignment to the colonies after her death, he participated in the capture of Charlestown in May 1780, and succeeded to command of the Southern Army. With inadequate funding and at the end of a tenuous supply line, Cornwallis was forced to supply his army by confiscation. He soon found himself ensnared in a partisan war for which his distinguished military career left him ill-prepared.

Cornwallis' talents did not extend to wise choices in subordinates. Distrust among his staff undermined Major Patrick Ferguson, an astute Scot who better understood how to deal with insurrection. Cornwallis instead placed implicit

An aggressive leader, Lieutenant-Colonel Banastre Tarleton was also reckless and cruel, and lied to Cornwallis to conceal his defeats. This copy of a portrait by Joshua Reynolds in the British Museum is romanticized. Fellow officers described Tarleton as pudgy and homely. (Anne S. K. Brown Collection)

trust in Banastre Tarleton, seeing in him what many senior officers lacked – a penchant for aggressive action.

**Lieutenant-Colonel Banastre Tarleton**'s aggression was usually unrestrained by logic, choosing attack even in the face of superior numbers and unfavorable tactical position. Twenty-six years old at the time of the battle of Cowpens, Tarleton has been praised as the finest cavalry leader on either side, and painted as a larger than life monster. Regardless of where the truth lies, it is important to understand how his reputation influenced the war in the south.

Son of a prominent merchant and mayor of Liverpool whose family fortune derived from West Indies plantations and slave trading, Tarleton never completed studies in law at Middle Temple. He inherited substantial wealth upon his father's death, but quickly squandered most on gambling and women. He purchased a cornet's commission in the First Dragoon Guards where he proved a talented horseman and leader, although obedience in the ranks was based mostly upon the instillation of fear of corporal punishment.

In December 1775 Tarleton traveled at his own expense to North America, where he participated in the failed British attempt to capture Charlestown (June 1776), and distinguished himself as an audacious cavalryman in the northern colonies. He quickly rose in rank to lieutenant-colonel through the approval of superiors rather than purchase of higher commissions. In 1778 several Loyalist formations were combined to form the British Legion, and sent south under Tarleton's command.

Tarleton burnished his reputation with a victory at Monck's Corner, South Carolina (April 14, 1780). In the aftermath a Legion trooper attempted to rape a local woman. Although the circumstances are murky, it marked the beginning of Tarleton's reputation for unwillingness to control the excesses of his subordinates.

Tarleton's reputation was irrevocably tarnished at The Waxhaws, though apologists for Tarleton and his Legion (beginning with Tarleton himself) have attempted to excuse their actions. A master of dissembling, Tarleton wrote that "a report amongst the cavalry, that they had lost their commanding officer … stimulated the soldiers to a vindictive asperity not easily restrained."

In fact Tarleton's men simply butchered surrendering rebels. American surgeon Robert Brownfield wrote that the Legion perpetrated "indiscriminate carnage never surpassed by the most ruthless atrocities of the most barbarous savages." The toll was 113 Patriots killed, 150 wounded too badly to be moved (most died), and 53 captured. The Legion's losses were seven killed and 13 wounded. (Most sources list 17 British casualties; our numbers are from a casualty return preserved in the British National Archives.) The Legion indiscriminately plundered and burned farms and properties, alienating the populace and driving many into active opposition as partisans.

Although Tarleton did act mercifully and honorably on occasion, stories of his barbarities are legion. In London after the war he "had the effrontery to boast, in the presence of a lady of respectability, that he had killed more men and ravished more women than any man in America." At one dead rebel general's plantation he purportedly had the cadaver exhumed and seated at the dinner

table, and forced the widow to serve the body a meal. Such tales may be apocryphal, but are consistent with documented murders, mutilations, and other atrocities. His foes grew increasingly eager to bring him down, and the avowed motivation of many Americans at Cowpens was personal revenge against Tarleton.

His reliance upon the skill and discipline of his infantry to carry the day against all odds led to disasters at Blackstock's Farm and Cowpens.

Born in 1730, **Major Archibald McArthur** joined the army at 17 and by 1781 was a very senior major when his 1st Battalion of the 71st Foot was subordinated to Tarleton. Although respected even by his enemies, promotion was slow. American General Charles Lee wrote that, unlike Tarleton, "no act of oppression or inhumanity ever attached to his name."

### British junior officers

Tarleton always overshadowed his subordinates, so little is known about most other than rudimentary biographical data and passing – often accusatory – mentions in his memoir. Part of the anonymity is also due to fearsome casualties among junior officers and NCOs in the British regiments. American marksmen targeted "cross-belts and epaulets," a practice that more than one British officer condemned as "damned unfair," although British and Hessian marksmen targeted American officers.

**Captain Richard Hovenden** was typical. One of three brothers who served in the British Legion, Richard was the only one present at Cowpens. He saw early service in the northern colonies, and commanded the scouts who first clashed with Morgan's pickets at Cowpens. A source for known information on British Legion officers is *The Online Institute for Advanced Loyalist Studies* (http://www.royalprovincial.com).

Attrition resulted in junior officers rising – and dying – quickly. **Lieutenant John Money** (another favorite of Cornwallis') was killed while leading the depleted 63rd Regiment of Foot at Blackstock's Farm. Tarleton reported this stinging defeat to Cornwallis as a great victory, and obliquely placed blame for casualties on Money, saying that the "ardor of the 63d had carried them too far."

# AMERICAN

An expert logistician, the "Quaker General" Nathanael Greene suffered from unending bad luck, but tactical defeats proved to be strategic victories. From a portrait by Charles Wilson Peale. (Anne S. K. Brown Collection)

**Nathanael Greene** was a general who lost battles but in so doing won the war. Self-educated in mathematics and law, he operated his family's foundry, and was active in politics. In 1774 he organized a local militia company, but met with resistance from rivals because of a limp; his militia activities also caused him to be voted out of his Quaker meeting house. Greene learned about war from books. A superb logistician and organizer, he rose to major-general in the Rhode Island Militia, was appointed to brigadier in the Continental Army, and was quickly promoted to major-general.

Greene served in a series of subordinate field commands, and won Washington's unshakeable confidence by his service as quartermaster general at Valley Forge in 1778. Greene continually clashed with members of Congress who meddled in Continental Army affairs because powerful New England members resented the appointment of a Virginian as commander-in-chief. Three Congressional appointees brought successive disasters in the south: Robert Howe lost Savannah, Benjamin Lincoln lost Charlestown, and Horatio Gates' blundering led to the debacle at Camden. When Congress finally allowed Washington to select a commander for the southern theater, he chose Greene without hesitation, making him second only to Washington in the command structure of the Continental Army.

In the south, Greene faced a situation that taxed his talents to the limit. In a region picked clean of supplies, the remnants of Gates' army supplied themselves by plundering the otherwise sympathetic populace. Weapons were in short supply, and in the face of the cruel winter of 1780/81 many of the starving men were barefoot, and some literally naked.

Patrick Ferguson's sizeable force of Loyalist militia had been totally destroyed at King's Mountain, and Tarleton defeated for the first time at Blackstock's Farm, but Cornwallis, Tarleton, and other British and Loyalist forces still rampaged through South Carolina. With Thomas Sumter wounded at Blackstock's, the South Carolina militia was in disarray, functioning as partisan bands that would somehow have to buy Greene precious time to rebuild the army.

On December 4, 1780 Greene relieved General Horatio Gates as commander of the Southern Department, as depicted by Howard Pyle. Gates' southern army was demoralized, starving, and some troops were naked. (Lodge)

The enigmatic **Daniel Morgan** was the self-made man of American myth. Large and physically strong, he ran away from home at 17, and concealed much about his origins. As a common laborer he amassed enough money to purchase a wagon and horses, and served as a teamster in the French and Indian War. He eventually became a soldier, rising through the ranks on the strength of a talent for fighting.

There are multiple versions of the first major incident of Morgan's military career. In the retreat from Braddock's Defeat (summer 1755) Morgan engaged in some sort of altercation with a British officer. Sentenced to 400 (or 500) lashes, normally a death sentence, by a miscount he received only 399 (or 499). The incident instilled an abiding hatred for the British officer class, and in later years Morgan would show his scars and say that the British "still owed him one." He was shot through the neck and mouth, leaving him with no left molars and a prominently scarred left cheek. After the war Morgan lived a frontier bachelor's life – drinking, gambling, and general carousing – until marriage reformed his ways.

By the 1770s Morgan was a thriving Virginia planter, and again served in the militia in Dunmore's War (1774) against the Shawnee. A friend of George Washington, he raised a company of riflemen and fought around Boston (1775–76). Morgan distinguished himself in the botched American attack on Quebec in late 1776. Captured and exchanged in January 1777, he was promoted to colonel and given command of the 11th Virginia Regiment of Continentals, and later the Provisional Rifle Corps.

Morgan again distinguished himself in the Saratoga battles (September 19 and October 7, 1777) that culminated in the surrender of most of British General John Burgoyne's army. At the surrender Burgoyne purportedly told Morgan that he commanded "the finest regiment in the world." Morgan grew disillusioned with a system in which connections in Congress counted for vastly more than ability, and high ranks and honors were lavished upon European volunteer officers who exhibited no particular talent. He resigned from the army at the end of June 1779.

Despite Gates' entreaties, Morgan declined to join the new Southern Army and avoided the Camden disaster. Morgan joined the beleaguered Southern Army in early October 1780 as commander of the light infantry, and was quickly promoted to brigadier-general. Morgan first met with Greene at Hillsborough, North Carolina on December 3, 1780.

Morgan "reflected deeply, spoke little" and led by example, traits much admired by the militia.

Prickly, ambitious, ever-mindful of status and perquisites, **Thomas Sumter** kept the fires of revolution alive during the Tory ascendancy of 1780. The obstreperous gamecock played no role at Cowpens, but in his capacity as brigadier-general in command of all South Carolina militia he repeatedly interfered, and often contradicted Greene and Morgan's orders. In turn, many of the independent-minded militia colonels felt free to ignore Sumter in their eagerness to have at Tarleton.

Brigadier-General Daniel Morgan habitually wore the hunting-garb of the militia. One of the great generals of American history, Morgan was likely the best tactician of the war. From a portrait by Alonzo Chappel. (NARA)

As commander of all South Carolina militia, Thomas Sumter constantly interfered with Greene and Morgan's operations. (Lossing)

The 38-year-old son of wealthy parents and (perhaps) second cousin of George Washington, **William Washington** had been privately tutored for the ministry. He joined the militia in February 1776, and later the 3rd Virginia Regiment of the Continental Line. After serving extensively in the northern colonies, he was sent south in command of the 3rd Light Dragoons in late 1779. After numerous costly defeats the depleted 1st and 3rd Light Dragoons were merged; after their colonel was captured, Washington assumed command. Assigned to Morgan's army, Washington's dragoons inflicted several defeats upon the British (often against superior forces), and his activities threatening the British base at Ninety Six were a key factor in Cornwallis' decision to assign Tarleton to hunt down Morgan. Most veterans considered Washington second-in-command to Morgan at Cowpens. Washington's dragoons played a key role by driving off Tarleton's dragoons at critical moments during the battle. Washington was captured at Eutaw Springs (September 8, 1781), and remained a prisoner until the end of the war. He went on to become a wealthy planter and horse-breeder, state legislator, and served again in the army in 1798 at George Washington's request.

**John Eager Howard** was the 28-year-old son of Maryland plantation owners. Commissioned as a captain in the Continental Line, by the time of Cowpens he was promoted to colonel of the veteran 2nd Maryland Regiment. Howard had a reputation for courage and coolness under fire, and Greene wrote that he was "as good an officer as the world affords."

Another Marylander, **Otho Howard Williams** was not at Cowpens. His leadership of Greene's light infantry during the Race to the Dan allowed Greene to preserve his army as a continuing threat to Cornwallis, thereby successfully exploiting the Cowpens victory.

**LEFT**
This painting of William Washington accurately depicts the Third Continental Dragoons uniform. Washington was notable for his tactical boldness and calm demeanor in battle. (Pamela Patrick White, www.whitehistoricart.com)

**RIGHT**
This period depiction of William Washington was less flattering; he was described by contemporaries as "six feet in height, broad, strong, and corpulent." (Lossing)

South Carolina militia forces were loosely organized, and as senior colonel the 41-year-old **Andrew Pickens** was regarded as the commander of the South Carolina militia at Cowpens. A devout Presbyterian, farmer, cattleman, and Indian trader, he was a veteran of service against the Cherokee, and against the British at Kettle Creek in 1779. After the fall of Charlestown, Pickens accepted parole, and served as a neutral commissioner to investigate the treatment of Loyalist prisoners taken at King's Mountain. When Loyalist raiders burned his farm and brutalized his family, he became a prominent partisan leader.

Although his battalion of militia, some of them veterans of service in the Continental Line, played a major role, little is known of their commander **Frank Triplett**. The term battalion causes considerable confusion, and some sources use the terms regiment and battalion interchangeably. In period usage a battalion was not a formal organizational term. Regiments were composed of companies, and when the regiment was subdivided for some reason the separated groups were called battalions. Triplett's rank – major – would indicate the usual practice of having a major command one of these separate battalions.

Commander of the largest militia contingent, **Colonel Thomas Brandon** was an affluent farmer, civic leader, and successful partisan commander. Shrewd and well regarded, and a veteran of much hard fighting, he often chose to subordinate his command to more ambitious leaders. Brandon had a reputation for relentless hatred of Loyalists, largely based on his killing of a prisoner who tried to escape with weapons after King's Mountain. However, he often pardoned Loyalist prisoners condemned to death, and was much admired by his men. His regiment secured the left flank of the militia line, most exposed to Tarleton's dreaded cavalry.

## Junior officers

Many officers down to company level have been extensively documented, and the list is too lengthy to summarize here. Details are covered in various works by Bobby Gilmer Moss, and summarized by Lawrence Babits (see *Further Reading*).

# OPPOSING FORCES

## AMERICAN

The American colonies had a tradition of militia service for local self-defense dating back to the original colonial charters. All free males were subject to conscription. Slaves and freedmen served as camp servants and fighting men, and members of friendly tribes like the Catawba served in the militia.

Militiamen were supposed to provide their own weapons, but at most about one in five was armed (see Gilbert and Gilbert, *Patriot Militiaman in the American Revolution, 1775–82*, Osprey Warrior 176). Militia duty, with its regular muster days and 90-day terms of service, kept men from their farms and trades, and was never popular. By the late 18th century it seemed burdensome but necessary, particularly along a frontier plagued by Cherokee and Creek raids. The militia of each state was under the control of the governor, who authorized formation of units and commissioned senior officers.

The populace of the colonies had a suspicion of standing armies that bordered on the pathological, since most were descendants of immigrants who had been oppressed by the armies of European monarchs. Experienced

**LEFT**
Contemporary depictions of American uniforms, like this one by German artist Christian Henning, are rare. Note the hunting shirt and trousers (in this case worn by Continentals), muskets with bayonets and cartouches (cartridge boxes), bare feet, and beards in an era when the fashion was to be clean-shaven. (Anne S. K. Brown Collection)

**RIGHT**
In reality, many Continentals like this light infantry rifleman wore extemporized uniforms, in this case a rough linen frock, locally made trousers, and sack moccasins. (Charles McBarron, Anne S. K. Brown Collection)

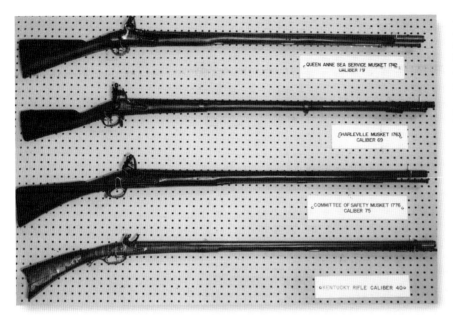

American troops used American, British, French, and German-made weapons. Shown here are (top to bottom) a British .79-caliber Queen Anne musket, French .69-caliber Charleville musket, American .75-caliber Committee of Safety musket, and American .40-caliber rifle. (USMC History Division)

soldiers like George Washington realized that disciplined regulars were necessary to counter the British Army, but the leaders of the new nation placed great emphasis on its "citizen soldiers."

The states that comprised the new republic functioned as semi-autonomous members of a confederation, and each raised their own State Troops. Many of the State Troops were absorbed into the Continental Army, but others remained under individual state control.

Morgan's army was a hodgepodge of all these various units. A detailed order of battle is available online at http://www.carolana.com/SC/Revolution/revolution_battle_of_cowpens.html, but the authors disagree with details and do not vouch for its correctness.

It is important to understand the discipline, weaponry, and capabilities of each, particularly the militia who comprised over 60 percent of Morgan's effectives.

### Continental Line Infantry
The hard core of Morgan's Flying Army was a battalion of veteran Continentals: three companies of the Maryland Line, and one company from Delaware. Highly trained and disciplined, they formed the main line under Howard. Continentals were armed with reliable Charleville military muskets that allowed rapid and consistent volley fire. Trained in the use of the bayonet, they were the troops best suited to engage in prolonged close combat with British regulars, and to resist the much-feared British dragoons. Morgan went to some pains to assure his militia that the Continentals would provide protection against Tarleton's dragoons.

Howard's Maryland Continentals ideally should have worn the standard uniform of the Continental Line. (Charles McBarron, Anne S. K. Brown Collection)

The Delaware Company was the most highly regarded, and most were survivors of the Camden debacle. Their commander, Captain Robert Kirkwood, was well regarded but never promoted to higher command. The three Maryland companies were survivors from several ravaged regiments. The First Company (Captain Richard Anderson) included survivors of the 1st and 7th Maryland. The Second Company (Captain Henry Dobson) was formed from the 2nd, 4th, and 6th Maryland. The Third Company (Lieutenant Nicholas Mangers) included men from the old 3rd and 5th Maryland.

## Continental dragoons

Dragoons served both sides as scouts, mounted pickets, mobile reserves, and shock troops. One of their primary functions was to exploit a victory by riding down the remnants of broken enemy infantry. Weaponry included a carbine and/or a brace of heavy pistols. Since firearms could not be quickly reloaded on horseback, their primary weapon was the saber.

## State Troops

These were local soldiers raised, uniformed, and equipped at the expense of the state, and similar to British Provincials. The infantry served enlistment of six to 18 months, were equipped with muskets and uniforms, and were better disciplined than short-service militia. Present at Cowpens were three companies of State Troops infantry from Virginia, North Carolina, and South Carolina. The Virginia contingent under Andrew Wallace included survivors of the Waxhaws Massacre. The handful of North Carolina infantry were primarily artisans and skilled laborers from the depot at Salisbury, North Carolina hastily sent south to reinforce Morgan. A handful of State Dragoons from Virginia, North Carolina, and South Carolina augmented Washington's Continentals.

## Virginia Militia battalions

Triplett's Virginia infantry battalion was something of an anomaly. Although short-enlistment militia, some were veterans of the Virginia Continental Line, so Morgan placed these reliable troops with his Continentals. An additional battalion of three companies was under Major David Campbell.

## South Carolina Militia Brigade

The largest contingent in Morgan's force was Pickens' brigade, several regiments of varying and indeterminate size. Given the numerical significance of the rebel militia, and the key role they played at Cowpens, it is important to examine these forces in detail.

Partisan tactics in the south forced both sides to rely heavily upon cavalry and mounted infantry. There were militia infantry units, but most militia functioned as mounted infantry carrying only a light bedroll behind the saddle. Tarleton's second in command, Major George Hanger, wrote:

> The crackers and militia in those parts of America are all mounted on horse-back, which renders it totally impossible to force them to an engagement with infantry only. When they chuse to fight, they dismount, and fasten their horses to the fences and rails; but if not very confident in the superiority of their numbers, they remain on horse-back, give their fire, and retreat, which renders it useless to attack them without cavalry: for though you repulse them, and drive them from the field, you never can improve the advantage, or do them any material detriment.

This print entitled *1st Virginia under Morgan* depicts a Continental, armed with a musket and belt knife in lieu of a bayonet. (US Army via NARA)

(Hanger was wounded at the battle of Charlotte on September 26, 1780, contracted yellow fever, and was evacuated to the Bahamas). Militia units had no fixed structure or strength. Regiments consisted of companies, but of variable number, and each company typically consisted of 20 to 40 men. Like regulars, militia regiments could be subdivided into battalions. Militiaman Adam Guyton stated that as a brigade, "Some times we had 75 some times 150 men, and some times we had 4 or 5 Cols with from 50 to 150 men. Each of them had Command of a Regt at home & some times not more than 5 of his men with him … we had no officer in our company & only two or three or four men." Lawrence Babits in *A Devil of a Whipping* provides one analysis of possible unit strengths and structures, and the problems inherent in trying to estimate unit strengths.

Dragoon pistols were massive, slow to reload, and fired only once in battle. The sturdy construction made them secondarily useful as clubs. This British pistol is 19in. (48cm) long. (USMC History Division)

Most militiamen were mounted infantry, but there were militia footmen. This militiaman is armed with a musket and wears a light marching pack. (Jeff Trexler, trexlerhistoricalart.com)

The present authors' estimate of the number of companies in militia regiments differs from other sources, but is based on pension records. At Cowpens the largest militia unit was likely Colonel Thomas Brandon's local Second Spartan Regiment of at least ten identified companies. Other units were Benjamin Roebuck's First Spartans (at least seven companies), the Little River Regiment under Lieutenant-Colonel Joseph Hayes (five companies), and the depleted First Spartan Regiment of Colonel John Thomas Junior (four known companies).

Two units illustrate the difficulty of assessing the role of militia. Many modern writers refer to the Second Spartans as the Fairforest Regiment, but the Fair Forest Regiment was a Loyalist militia regiment. The Second Spartans were formed when the original Spartan Regiment was divided in 1778, recruited from the "Brown's Creek Irish" settlements, and their headquarters was not relocated to a blockhouse on Fair Forest Creek until 1781. Contemporary records referred to the Spartan Regiment, Second Division. The members referred to it as the Second Spartans, Lower Spartans, or most commonly as Brandon's Regiment. Thomas was commissioned in the State Troops in December, but returned to lead the new Colonel (Benjamin Roebuck's) First Spartans at Cowpens.

Militia regiments were mostly fighting on their home ground at Cowpens, so men continued to unofficially attach themselves to regiments until the very last hours before the battle, and some fought as individuals. It was these late arrivals who forced Morgan to repeatedly revise his battle plan. Some men with better mounts were hastily issued swords and served as scouts, pickets, and dragoons in Washington's command. It is impossible to determine the true strength of any of these units.

Senior officers served continuously, but enlisted men were volunteers or conscripts who served short enlistments, usually 90 days. When numbers of volunteers were insufficient, junior officers scoured the regiment's recruiting district, conscripting known Whigs. Conscripts were usually young unmarried men; those with skilled trades were sometimes excused, and the more affluent

It was a fairly common practice to cut down the length of the barrel to make dragoon pistols more manageable. (Authors' photograph)

could hire substitutes. Many men served multiple voluntary enlistments: active militia service was safer when your Loyalist neighbors were likely to murder you. Many were experienced albeit reluctant soldiers, and Private Charles Gilbert (no known relationship to the authors) stated that over a period of two years, nine months he received only three "short furloughs," and "so urgent was the necessities of the Country during the whole of the above period that this declarant was at no time permitted to follow any civil pursuit."

The militia was equipped with a bewildering variety of captured or scavenged weaponry that rendered standardized drill or sustained volley fire impossible. Poorly disciplined, they had a tendency to desert in order to protect their families and property. The militia was deemed ill-disciplined and unreliable, and at the bottom of the military pecking order; Morgan, a former militiaman, did not place much faith in them.

Before the battle of Camden Horatio Gates scorned the services of Francis Marion's militia scouts because "most of them [were] miserably equipped; their appearance was in fact so burlesque, that it was with much difficulty the diversion of the regular soldiery was restrained by the officers." The appearance of Marion's command was so lacking in military appearance that Gates "was glad of an opportunity of detaching Colonel Marion, at his own instance, toward the interior of South Carolina." Morgan would not repeat that mistake.

## Georgia refugee militia

Driven out of Georgia after the fall of Savannah, these die-hards fought on in South Carolina, typically operating in conjunction with various South Carolina militia regiments. Some of the Georgia men volunteered to augment the dragoons.

**LEFT**
A Virginia rifleman; note the recognition symbol on the hat. (US Army via NARA)

**RIGHT**
This militiaman depicted by Steve Noon wears hunting garb over a linen shirt, and is armed with an expensive small-bore rifle. Note the paper tucked into the hatband as a recognition symbol. (Gilbert and Gilbert)

### Militia dragoons

One of Morgan's greatest concerns was his lack of adequate numbers of dragoons. Several small militia contingents augmented Washington's force. Thomas Young was a militiaman in the Second Spartan Regiment who answered the last-minute call:

> It was all important to strengthen the cavalry. Gen. Morgan knew well the power of Tarleton's legion, and he was too wily an officer not to prepare himself as well as circumstances would admit. Two companies of volunteers were called for. One was raised by Major Jolly of Union District, and the other, I think, by Major McCall. [The remainder of McCall's battalion was attached to Major Samuel Hammond's State Troops as skirmishers.] I attached myself to Major Jolly's company. We drew swords that night, and were informed we had authority to press any horse not belonging to a dragoon or an officer, into our service for the day.

In summary, there are as many estimates of Morgan's troop strength as there are writers about Cowpens, ranging from fewer than 800 to over 2,500. An early estimate may well be the handwritten sum on the lower margin of the so-called "Pigree map" preserved in the National Archives – 889 – but that is a small and suspiciously precise number. Henry Wells of the Delaware Company recalled fewer than 900, mostly militia, with "less than 100 horse." With the exception of the Continentals and State Troops, the estimates below should not be taken very seriously.

### Support and transport

Continentals and State Troops operated at the far limits of a tenuous supply system that was irregularly funded by a stingy Congress. They did not possess the lavish equipment of their British counterparts, and tended to make less use of horse-drawn transport.

A major problem for the rebel militia was the bewildering variety of firearms: French Charleville military muskets; numerous types of captured

Light artillery carriages were traditionally painted blue. This weapon is a light howitzer of the 4th South Carolina Artillery, but shows the details of the weapon carriage and associated equipment. The tampion protected the muzzle from water and debris. In action the crew pushed or pulled the weapon to accompany the infantry. (Authors' photograph)

British and German weapons; fowling pieces (shotguns); rifles and muskets manufactured under Congressional contracts; prewar civilian rifles, muskets, and shotguns; and dozens of types of pistols. The variety of types and calibers forced individuals or small groups to mold their own projectiles. The American militias in particular suffered from chronic shortages of powder and lead, sometimes forcing substitution of pewter for lead.

The militia of both sides, operating close to home, tended to carry minimal supplies or equipment, with the exception of some senior officers who had camp equipment and servants or slaves. Period accounts describe the occasional militia use of tents provided from government sources.

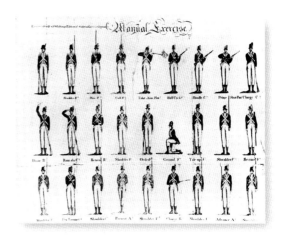

Morgan's Continentals were trained according to Steuben's drill manual and unlike militia could stand up to the disciplined British Redcoats. (NARA)

| Morgan's approximate troop strength | |
| --- | --- |
| Continental Battalion | 300 |
| State Troops – Virginia | 75 |
| State Troops – North Carolina | (no records) |
| State Troops – South Carolina | 60 |
| South Carolina Militia | 730 |
| Triplett's Virginia Militia Battalion | 160 |
| Virginia Militia | 50 |
| North Carolina Militia | 285 |
| Georgia refugees | 55 |
| Continental Dragoons | 82 |
| North Carolina and Virginia Stage Dragoons | 30 |
| South Carolina Stage Dragoons | 25 |
| Local Militia Dragoons | 45 |
| **Total** | **1,897** |

Morgan's Flying Army made only limited use of wheeled transport, more typically drawn by horses in the South. The British were more dependent upon transport, and shortages of horses often hobbled operations. (*Harper's Weekly*)

# BRITISH

On the whole the officers of the British Southern Army were typical of the country's officer class. The enlisted men of the British forces in the southern colonies consisted of four general categories: "Redcoat" regulars, "Hessian mercenaries," Provincials, and local militia.

Regular regiments comprised long-service soldiers, usually recruited from the lower rungs of British society and subjected to harsh – sometimes deadly – discipline. Britain began the war with units raised in England, Scotland, and Ireland, but by 1781 heavy losses from disease and combat had severely bled most formations. Britain was also enmeshed in a global war, with the need to defend more lucrative (and far less troublesome) colonies in the Caribbean and around the globe. The perceived solution was increasing enlistment of colonials to fill the depleted ranks of regular regiments.

Not all enlistments were entirely voluntary. Captured rebels were often given the option of enlisting in British service. The alternatives were confinement in local jails at places like Ninety Six, where prisoners subsisted on the leavings of the garrison's horses, or the even more horrific prison hulks anchored in Charlestown Harbor. Prison conditions were so ghastly that as much as 40 percent of all American military deaths occurred while in British captivity. William Dunn sailed from England as a cabin boy, jumped ship in Virginia, and eventually enlisted in the Continentals. Captured at Camden, "his only alternative appeared to be an enlistment in the British service with a prospect of deserting them and again joining the American Army, or starvation as a prisoner – he chose the first." Dunn deserted, found some of his old comrades, and fought the British again at Cowpens.

Highly disciplined, the regular infantry were skilled with the bayonet as a primary weapon. The British regiments that served in North America were trained in skills that differed from their counterparts in European service, and in fact differed from those employed in the northern colonies. Infantry were drilled in orthodox European tactics that required considerable training and discipline. The infantry were trained to fight in close order, standing shoulder to shoulder in dense formations that maximized firepower. In open order men advanced with a spacing of several yards between individuals, allowing easier movement through forested or rough terrain. In extended order men might be separated by as much as 150ft (45m), and units were trained to shift from one formation to another fairly quickly.

Many regiments included a grenadier company of heavy shock infantry; these were seldom used in the southern colonies,

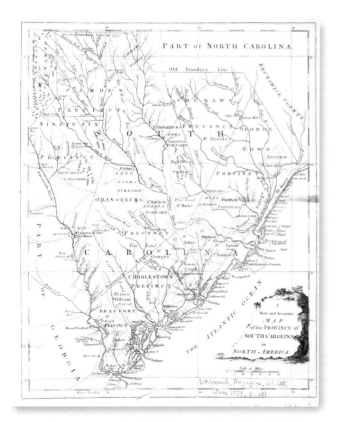

The few roads in South Carolina limited military operations. "Detailed" maps like this 1779 depiction were not available to the combatants. (Library of Congress)

though the distinctive helmets figure prominently in romanticized art. More important were the light infantry companies, with men selected for intelligence and initiative. These troops were lightly equipped, fast-moving infantry trained as scouts and skirmishers, often skilled marksmen, and often operated independently of parent formations.

When confronted by local militia armed with rifles but not trained or equipped for close combat, British tactics were to "charge the fire," firing one or two volleys then charging with the bayonet. Contending with rebel mounted militia led to the extensive use of mounted infantry who rode to battle but fought on foot. These formations were usually extemporized, with infantrymen temporarily mounted on seized farm horses. The fluid war also lent greater importance to dragoons, or light cavalry. Dragoons were the troops best suited to deal with the mounted partisans, who in general were not equipped with sabers and pistols for mounted combat.

When recruiting efforts could not meet the demand for soldiers, the British government rented soldiers from German princely states, generally lumped together as "Hessians" (large numbers came from the German state of Hesse). They were not true mercenaries; their prince profited while the troops were paid a pittance. German regiments also included light infantry companies called jaegers (hunters).

Provincials or uniformed militia were long-enlistment colonials, equipped as best British logistical problems allowed, and sometimes trained and disciplined to the standards of regulars. The rebels tended to lump these units with the long-service regulars and referred to both as "Redcoats."

Loyalist militias were short-service locals, clothed in civilian garb like their opposite numbers in the rebel militias, and equipped with a hodgepodge of British-supplied arms. The Loyalist militias included men who had their own scores to settle with the rebel militias, usually arising from loss of property to plunder or confiscation, or atrocities committed by rebel fanatics.

Loyalist militia officers, though some were promoted as high as brigadier-general, never had the status of Crown officers and in fact their orders could be countermanded by junior British officers. Regular officers scorned the militia, and before the war one British officer described the militia as led by "Blacksmiths, Taylors and all the Banditti the country affords." Patrick Ferguson urged Cornwallis to appoint militia officers on the basis of merit, but Cornwallis preferred "men of property and substance." (Ferguson was meritoriously promoted to lieutenant-colonel, but upon his appointment as Inspector of Militia was reduced in rank to major, considered a grade more commensurate with command of militia.) Some were able leaders, but all too many failed miserably when pitted against talented rebel commanders.

Although they played no part at Cowpens, the British armed the colonists' long-standing foes, the Cherokee and Creek tribes. This was another practice that infuriated the rebels, but for the British it had the strategic advantage of forcing the Americans to fight a savage second-front war along the mountainous frontier.

### The British Legion

Formed in July 1778 by Sir Henry Clinton, the Legion merged bits and pieces of several existing Provincial formations. The term Legion indicated a combined-arms brigade, with light infantry, cavalry, and a small detachment of mobile artillery, and was intended for fast-moving operations and raiding.

The Legion included colonists from the Royal American Reformers, West Jersey Volunteers, Roman Catholic Volunteers, New York Dragoons, Philadelphia Light Dragoons, Emmerich's Chasseurs, Prince of Wales' American Volunteers, 16th Light Dragoons, and later the Bucks County Dragoons, all from the New York–New Jersey–Philadelphia region. The commanding officer was Colonel Lord William Cathcart, with Banastre Tarleton as lieutenant-colonel. When the Legion was sent south, Cathcart remained in New York and Tarleton assumed field command, but was never promoted to the colonelcy. The Legion later incorporated Loyalists from Georgia, as indicated by recruiting notices. The ranks were further filled by former prisoners. The journal of Loyalist Alexander Chesney described Tarleton's "Regiment of Cavalry called the British Legion which was filled up from the prisoners taken at the battle of Camden."

The Legion was undoubtedly proficient at terrorizing the populace, and was much feared and hated by the Patriots. As might be expected of political zealots in a partisan war, the Legion quickly developed a reputation for arson, plunder, rape, torture, and indiscriminate murder. Tarleton's favored Green Dragoons did not perform with any distinction when confronted by enemies determined to fight. The turncoats of the Legion who had engaged in repeated depredations against the families of Patriots were understandably loath to fall into enemy hands, and at Cowpens fled the field rather than risk possible capture and execution.

### 1st Battalion, 71st Regiment of Foot

The 71st was raised in 1775 specifically for service in America, under many veteran officers. About two-thirds of the recruits were Scots, and though often called Fraser's Highlanders, the title was not official and in fact many of the recruits were lowland Scots. After service in the northern colonies, the regiment was sent south in December 1778. From that time forward all or parts of the regiment were involved in most of the actions of the southern campaign. The 71st had incorporated numerous colonial recruits, though the morale of the unit as a regular regiment was high.

The 1st Battalion under Major Archibald McArthur was assigned to Tarleton's command to pursue Daniel Morgan's Flying Army until the clash at Cowpens. The only men to escape the Cowpens debacle were those few left guarding the baggage trains in the rear. As a result of the defeat the regiment thereafter wore no uniform facings. The officers of the 71st petitioned Cornwallis that the regiment never again serve under Tarleton's command, and Cornwallis honored the request. The remnants of the 71st Foot fought on, and surrendered at Yorktown.

### 17th Light Dragoons

Formed in 1759, the regiment was sent to Boston in 1775 to help quell the growing rebellion. Only a small part of the regiment was sent south, attached to Tarleton's command, but they clung to the by now bedraggled scarlet coats that set them apart from the green-clad Provincials of the Legion. Only about a hundred dragoons survived by the time of the Cowpens battle. It was the only unit to retire from the battlefield in good order.

### 7th Royal Fusiliers

As indicated by the name the 7th was formed as an escort to the Royal Artillery. Based in Canada prior to the Revolution, the regiment was

essentially destroyed in the 1775–76 American invasion. Re-formed in late 1776 from exchanged prisoners, the regiment fought in the northern colonies until sent south in 1779. The Fusiliers formed part of the Charlestown garrison before being moved to Winnsboro. Like many units, "the Regiment was not at the highest state of efficiency; it had suffered heavily from disease, and the few men who represented it were almost entirely recruits." At Cowpens this was evident when men fired prematurely, or broke ranks to pursue the "fleeing" American militia. Tarleton laid part of the blame for the Cowpens debacle on the "inexperienced" 7th, but as quoted in the history of the Fusiliers, an American officer present at Cowpens said: "the Fusiliers … had served with credit in America from the commencement of the war, and under an excellent officer, General Clark, had attained the summit of military discipline." The 7th must have fought well, as disproportionate numbers of Patriot casualties were suffered by formations who faced the 7th Fusiliers.

The 71st Foot had proven one of Cornwallis' most reliable units in battles like Brier Creek (March 3, 1779). The 1st Battalion was virtually destroyed at Cowpens. (Jeff Trexler, trexlerhistoricalart.com)

## Light infantry

Tarleton's light infantry force was an amalgam of two small detachments, the light companies of the 16th Foot and the Prince of Wales' American Regiment. The 16th was a regular regiment originally based in East Florida, and fought at Savannah. The Prince of Wales' American Regiment was raised in Connecticut in 1776, and fought in the northern colonies until sent south in May 1778. Additional recruits were enlisted in Charlestown, including 50 from the Loyalist Volunteers of Ireland. The Prince of Wales' American Regiment fought bravely and effectively, but was badly mauled by American militia at Hanging Rock (August 6, 1780). Most of the unit was captured at Cowpens, and only a handful were exchanged or paroled.

### Royal Artillery

The Legion artillery consisted of two 3-pdr (47mm) "grasshopper guns," with two dozen (some sources say up to 50) crewmen distinguished by blue uniform jackets with red facings, quite similar to the uniform of American Continental infantrymen. Properly used, the guns should have given Tarleton a pronounced tactical advantage.

The guns were towed by horses for rapid movement, but in action were wheeled into position by the crews. In an orthodox action the guns would be used to soften up the enemy line, and then pushed forward, firing as they advanced. Artillery of this small caliber usually fired solid shot – iron balls that plowed through formations, dismembering and demoralizing infantry.

Tarleton's attack at Cowpens was so hasty that he did not take advantage of his artillery's potential. True to the traditions of the artillery, the gunners at Cowpens by Patriot accounts fought valiantly to defend their guns against the counterattack until overwhelmed.

### Loyalist militia

Tarleton possessed even more than the usual British regular officers' disdain for militia, and had only a small contingent serving as spies (scouts) and guides.

Tarleton's 3-pdr. "grasshopper guns" like this reproduction at the Cowpens National Military Park provided him with a tremendous tactical advantage. Note the leather straps securing the tampion and rear of the gun tube. (Authors' photograph)

## Support and transport

Transport is a limitation seldom considered by historians, but was an overarching concern for the British in the south. British army regulations called for each infantry regiment to be supported by four heavy wagons drawn by 16 horses. Operating in sparsely settled and often hostile territory, transport was augmented by impressed wagons, or by wagons and teams operated by sympathizers or civilian contractors. These baggage trains carried food, tents, basic camp necessities, and ammunition. British officers traveled in luxury, with furniture, wine, crystal, silverware, and china, and sometimes women carried on the rolls as laundresses. Other accounts describe such necessities as traveling forges to shoe the numerous horses and repair weapons, ambulances, and extra weapons. Period accounts also mention trains of camp followers – women or entire families.

The resupply of isolated garrisons necessitated cumbersome supply convoys, and escorts for these convoys absorbed considerable manpower. British transport problems were further exacerbated by the systematic seizure of any available horses and wagons by American partisans.

**Tarleton's approximate troop strength**

| | |
|---|---|
| 71st Foot | 334 |
| Legion dragoons | 250 |
| Legion infantry | 200 |
| 7th Fusiliers | 176 |
| Loyalist militia | 50 |
| 17th Light Dragoons | 100 |
| 16th Foot Light Infantry | 42 |
| Prince of Wales' Light Infantry | 31 |
| Royal Artillery | 24 |
| **Total:** | **1,207** |

Henry Wells (the Continental Delaware Company) stated that "[Tarleton] outnumbered us in infantry and had three or four times as many Cavalry." Although by most accounts Morgan's force was superior in numbers, Tarleton's force should have possessed, and in his mind certainly did possess, the advantage because of superior training, discipline, weaponry, and experience. What Tarleton failed to take into account was Morgan's careful planning, and the great intangible: the American militia's hatred of Tarleton himself.

# OPPOSING PLANS

The overarching strategic goals of Cornwallis and Greene were simple, but almost impossible for either to achieve.

Cornwallis' mission was to subdue the Carolinas and sweep north into Virginia, a rich, populous, and largely unscathed colony that supplied rebel recruits and leadership in inordinate abundance. The Delmarva Peninsula, east of Chesapeake Bay, shared by Delaware, Maryland, and Virginia, was called "the breadbasket of the Revolution."

The absolutely necessary first step was to suppress the rebellion in South Carolina, but unexpectedly tenacious rebel partisans thwarted that goal. With limited forces, Cornwallis was reduced to a strategy of holding the strategic ports of Charlestown and Savannah, and the lesser ports of Beaufort in South Carolina and Wilmington in North Carolina. Inland positions at Ninety Six (a road nexus) and Camden were seen as key positions protecting all-important Charlestown. Another strategic position was Augusta, Georgia, a trading gateway to the Cherokee and Creeks.

In late September 1780 Cornwallis advanced into North Carolina, shadowed by rebel partisans under William R. Davie. On September 26 Tarleton was ill with a fever, and Major George Hanger let the British Legion

Most residents of the back country lived in cabins far more primitive than this replica at King's Mountain State Park, South Carolina. (Authors' photograph)

Cornwallis' screen and the invasion of North Carolina, 1780.

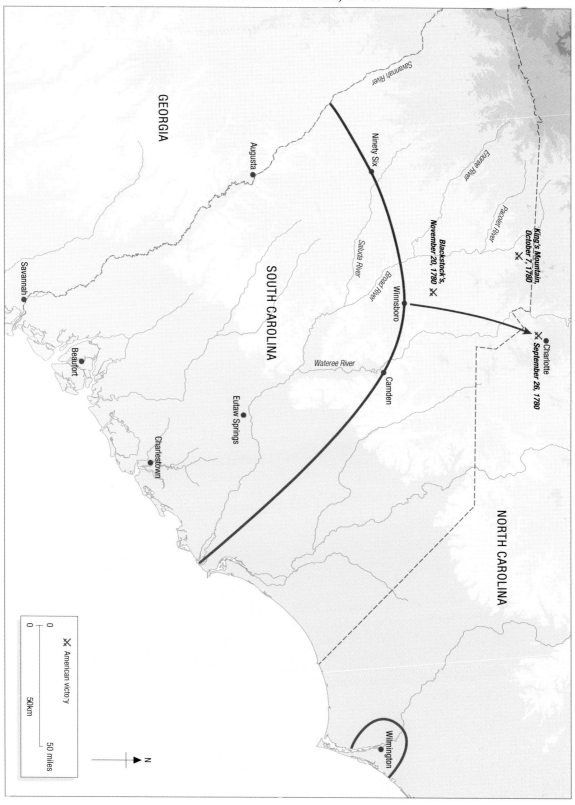

GEORGIA

Augusta

Savannah

Beaufort

Charlestown

Eutaw Springs

SOUTH CAROLINA

Ninety Six

Saluda River

Broad River

Wateree River

Winnsboro

Camden

Savannah River

Enoree River

Pacolet River

King's Mountain, October 7, 1780

Blackstock's, November 20, 1780

Charlotte September 26, 1780

NORTH CAROLINA

Wilmington

American victory

0
0
50km
50 miles

N

dragoons be drawn into a small but vicious battle in the small town of Charlotte, North Carolina. The battle was, in Hanger's words, "a trifling insignificant skirmish," but it indicated a rebel determination to resist Cornwallis' northward march. Rebel resistance stiffened, partisans plagued British foraging parties, and Cornwallis delayed his plans to march on his next objective, Salisbury, the seat of the North Carolina government and a major American supply depot.

To screen his inland flank, Cornwallis sent Major Patrick Ferguson on a two-fold mission. Foremost was a recruiting sweep southwest from Charlotte into the South Carolina back country. The second was to forestall any threat from the Scots-Irish communities on the western slope of the Appalachians, called "back water" towns because the local streams flowed westward.

That effort failed miserably. In his early service in Rhode Island Ferguson advocated wholesale destruction of towns and farms, but in the south acquired a reputation for trying to woo rebels back to the royal cause by persuasion. Thus far the "back water men," under threat from Cherokee raids, had largely sat out the war. Uncharacteristically, Ferguson sent word to the over-mountain settlements that "if they did not desist from their opposition to the British arms, he would march his army over the mountains, hang their leaders, and lay their country waste with fire and sword."

The threat backfired. A large force of over-mountain militia assembled and crossed the mountains to eliminate Ferguson. On October 7, 1780 Ferguson was trapped at King's Mountain and killed, and almost his entire command of 1,100 militia and Provincials killed or captured. On November 20 the hard-charging Tarleton trapped Sumter's militia brigade with its back to the Tyger River at Blackstock's Farm, only to suffer a stunning defeat that Tarleton, in his usual fashion, reported to Cornwallis as a great victory.

King's Mountain and the upwelling of militia activity in the wake of Blackstock's Farm forced Cornwallis to break off his invasion of North Carolina and return south to deal with the rapidly deteriorating situation. He established his main bases in and around the road nexus at Winnsboro to refit, absorb replacements, and prepare for the coming winter.

The remnants of the American southern army under Horatio Gates occupied Charlotte. The army was starving, and a smallpox epidemic ravaged the town. Newly assigned Nathanael Greene relieved Gates and assumed command of the remnant of the southern army at Hillsborough, North Carolina on December 3, 1780.

Even before Greene's arrival, Morgan and the light troops – about 300 infantry and William Washington's 80 or so dragoons – had been plaguing Cornwallis. This relatively powerful force was to escort foraging parties seeking meat and grain, but incidentally forced Loyalists out of the field and back into their local garrisons.

British hopes in the South were dealt a stunning blow by the destruction of Patrick Ferguson's Loyalist militia command at King's Mountain, October 7, 1780. (Authors' photograph)

While partisans distracted Cornwallis, Greene, the master of planning, set about reorganizing and re-equipping his army. He also dispatched officers to map and familiarize themselves with the military geography (particularly roads and the river crossings that were major chokepoints), select potential campsites, and assess the logistical situation. The stage was being meticulously set for the climactic phase of the war in the south.

Greene's overarching strategic mission, simply stated, was to survive. So long as Greene retained an active army-in-being, Cornwallis could not abandon the Carolinas with rebel partisans running rampant and a rebel army at his back. Greene's plans were to threaten, annoy, and distract Cornwallis, instructions which he passed on to Daniel Morgan in a dispatch dated January 8, 1781:

> If you employ detachments to intercept supplies going to Ninety-Six and Augusta, it will perplex the enemy very much. If you think Ninety-Six, Augusta or even Savannah can be surprised … you may attempt it. But don't think of attempting either unless by surprise … If you could detach a small party to kill the enemy's draught horses and recruiting cavalry upon the Congaree [River], it would give them almost as deadly a blow as a defeat.

Morgan was acting independently because Greene had been forced by circumstances to violate a fundamental military tenet: he had divided his small army.

The activities of both armies were increasingly controlled by that bane of all military endeavors, logistics – in this case, shortages of food for soldiers and fodder for animals. Years of foraging armies, raiding, plundering, and disruption of farming activities had depleted the countryside of food. Horses were in short supply – hence Greene's admonition about killing horses. Greene's isolated army could expect little in the way of support from Congress. Under no circumstances could he supply a large enough force to be assured of victory over Cornwallis, and the American cause could ill afford another southern disaster. Dividing his force to distract Cornwallis was the only way Greene could exploit the King's Mountain victory.

Both sides adopted positions from which they would be able to quickly combine separate forces if opportunity presented itself. But given the roads – few, poor, and mostly unmapped – this was more a dream than a practical possibility. Cornwallis positioned his main force at Winnsboro, South Carolina in part because local roads offered better communications, in part because the region to the south had not been so heavily plundered.

On December 20 Greene marched south from Charlotte, and on December 25 reached a preselected position on Hick's Creek just across

Immediately prior to Cowpens, Tarleton engaged in a futile pursuit of Francis Marion and his guerrillas in the eastern lowlands. Marion made skilled use of the terrain, as in William T. Ranney's *Marion Crossing the Pee Dee*. (Anne S. K. Brown Collection)

the Pee Dee River from the small town of Cheraw. On December 21 Morgan departed Charlotte for a position on the Pacolet River at Grindal Shoals.

Cornwallis had some logistical advantages in that he could be resupplied by sea. However, by early 1781 British naval transport, both from England and along the coast of North America, was prey to French warships, the tiny American Navy, and privateers. Once at the colonial ports, lack of transport, bad roads, and unrelenting attacks by the likes of Francis Marion made the safe passage of any supply column chancy. Cornwallis' preserved correspondence records bombardment by letters complaining of ever-increasing depredations by rebel partisan bands that commandeered horses, wagons, and whatever meager supplies that might be assembled by Loyalist sympathizers. Even the hard-charging Tarleton was increasingly obsessed with foraging.

Cornwallis was also faced with a dilemma posed by accidentally congruent rebel strategies. In the back country the partisans operated in large bands, threatening bases like Ninety Six. Near the coast guerrillas (a word that did not yet exist) plagued British lines of communication and supply, and threatened bases like Camden. Greene had unleashed Lieutenant-Colonel Henry "Light Horse Harry" Lee and his Continental dragoons to cooperate with Francis Marion's guerrillas in the low country. Unlike Brigadier-General Thomas Sumter, Marion had no qualms about working with Greene. Most of these attacks were pinpricks, but they weighed heavily upon Cornwallis' mind. Should he concentrate units to deal with the large rebel forces, or disperse to pursue raiders and defend outposts?

In turn, British and Loyalist partisan patrols continued to ravage the countryside, particularly Major James Dunlap operating out of Ninety Six. In one incident recorded in detail, a Loyalist patrol searching for a father and son found instead a cousin, badly wounded at King's Mountain. They dragged the man into the yard, but one Loyalist argued, "Let him alone, he will die in a few days any how." They plundered the home, taking food, destroying furnishings, seizing or destroying all the bedding and clothing, a particular hardship in the bitter winter. They threatened to kill Ann Kennedy, the young woman left in charge of the household, and broke her hand when she resisted.

Eventually "a few resolute whig women assembled together and wrote a note to General Morgan … to send a company to Union to subdue the tories, but no one manifested a willingness to be the bearer of the note, until Miss Ann Kennedy stepped up and volunteered her services to carry it. She concealed the note in her stocking – pinned a sunbonnet around her head – mounted a pony – rode about sixty miles – delivered the note to General Morgan and returned home in safety."

When Washington received word that the Loyalist Fair Forest Militia was burning Patriot homes, abusing and robbing families, he set off deep into Loyalist territory with 84 dragoons and some mounted militiamen. Washington's dragoons and about 20 mounted militia from the Second Spartans approached the Loyalist position at Rugeley's Fort – a fortified log barn – on December 4, 1780. Washington's men had no chance of capturing a strong position held by an equal force of Loyalist militia. Mounting a log on wheels to simulate a cannon, Washington put on a martial display and sent an emissary to demand immediate surrender. Colonel Henry Rugeley complied. Washington burned the fort and left with valuable horses, a wagon to transport captured muskets (other wagons were burned), and 114 prisoners.

In the low country Marion's patrols continued to terrorize small Loyalist garrisons, but suffered a rare defeat at Halfway Swamp on December 13.

When Washington caught up with Colonel Thomas Waters' Loyalists at Hammond's Old Store on December 27, the enemy had chosen a strong defensive position. Patriot militiaman Thomas Young wrote:

> we perceived that the Tories had formed in line on the brow of the hill opposite us. We had a long hill to descend another to rise. Col. Washington and his dragoons gave a shout, drew swords and charged down the hill like madmen. The Tories fled in every direction without firing a gun. We took a great many prisoners and killed a few.

The Americans, enraged by Waters' atrocities, held nothing back. By most accounts about 150 Loyalists were killed or wounded, 40 or so captured.

After South Carolina militia Colonel James Williams was killed at King's Mountain, Loyalist Colonel Moses Kirkland evicted Williams' widow and small children, confiscated his property, and fortified the main house, locally known as Williams' Fort. On New Year's Eve a handful of Washington's dragoons and Little River militia under Colonel Joseph Hayes imperiously demanded the surrender of the far larger Loyalist garrison under Brigadier-General Robert Cunningham, cousin of infamous Loyalist Colonel William "Bloody Bill" Cunningham. While Cunningham dickered over terms, most of his garrison slipped away. Hayes took a few prisoners, carried away all the military stores he could carry, and burned the stockade and remaining supplies.

These were minor pinpricks to British power, but they fueled Cornwallis' growing anxiety for the safety of his linchpin, the fort at Ninety Six.

Morgan was not idle in camp. He was seeking a better understanding of his most dangerous foe, quizzing militia leaders who had faced Tarleton. Colonel Richard Winn among others advised Morgan that "His mode of fighting is surprise. By [way of] doing this he sends two or three troops of horse, and, if he can throw the party into confusion, with his reserve he falls on [them and] will cut them to pieces."

Marion's guerrillas plagued British communications, forced dispersal of effort, and freed captives to fight again, as depicted in this Currier and Ives print. (Anne S. K. Brown Collection)

Cornwallis finally decided to eliminate Morgan. Unaware that Morgan's instructions were to avoid battle and that he wanted to move south to threaten Georgia, Cornwallis sent word to Tarleton to break off his futile pursuit of the "Swamp Fox" Marion and move northwest. Cornwallis, with the main army, would maneuver into a position to block rebel forces from withdrawing into North Carolina, and where he could wait to link up with Major-General Alexander Leslie's newly arrived reinforcements from Ireland, then marching slowly from Charlestown toward Camden.

Cornwallis wrote Tarleton:

> [I] desire you would pass Broad river, with the legion and the first battalion of the 71st, as soon as possible. If Morgan is still at Williams', or any where within your reach, I should wish you to push him to the utmost: I have not heard, except from M'Arthur, of his having cannon; nor would I believe it, unless he has it from very good authority: It is, however, possible, and Ninety Six is of so much consequence, that no time is to be lost.

To speed his pursuit, Tarleton asked Cornwallis for more transport wagons and light troops. He ordered that no women were to accompany his baggage trains, but retained baggage that would allow his officers to maintain their lifestyle.

Unfortunately for Cornwallis the winter weather interfered with his careful plans. Torrential rains flooded the lowland river crossings, delaying Leslie's march. Cornwallis lingered while Tarleton and Morgan moved steadily away.

## THE FORCES CONVERGE

Greene, aided by the weather, pursued his strategic goal of pinning Cornwallis in place. Under his command the main army would move south, to threaten the British base at Camden, but in reality avoiding battle. The Flying Army under Morgan would move west, threatening Ninety Six and Augusta. In the vernacular of the era a flying army was a mobile force of cavalry and infantry, kept in constant motion in order to distract and discomfit the enemy. Morgan would, if possible, draw Tarleton and Cornwallis into the back country.

Tarleton sent messengers asking Cornwallis to move into position near Hannah's Cowpens to threaten Morgan's rear, but Cornwallis was still trying to link up with Leslie and deal with Greene's threat. He advised Tarleton that the rain-swollen rivers had delayed the reinforcements, so Tarleton did not have any reason to expect Cornwallis would immediately march to his support. As usual a precarious situation would not dissuade Tarleton in the least.

A battalion of four companies from the 7th Fusiliers under Major Newmarsh and a detachment of the 17th Light Dragoons were escorting a supply train to Tarleton. The Fusilier battalion, a skeleton force with nine officers and 167 men, was supposed to continue on to reinforce the Ninety Six garrison. Tarleton received reports of Morgan's growing strength, and Cornwallis granted permission to attach the Fusiliers and Dragoons to his command.

On January 12 Andrew Pickens, camped at Fair Forest Meeting House, was notified by his scouts that Tarleton was on the move. On January 13 Greene dispatched a letter to Morgan warning that "Col. Tarleton is said to be on his way to pay you a visit."

On January 14 Tarleton learned that Morgan had placed outposts on all fords of the Pacolet River, that Leslie was at last able to move past the flooded rivers above Charlestown, and as a consequence that Cornwallis had begun to move slowly north. Deducing that Morgan would try to retreat into North Carolina, Tarleton asked Cornwallis to move up the east bank of the Broad River to cut off that line of retreat.

On January 15 Tarleton forced a crossing of the Pacolet, and by late morning occupied a position in some log houses in case Morgan attacked. That night Tarleton learned from a prisoner that Morgan had instead "struck into byways, tending towards Thickelle [Thicketty] Creek," and that a strong force of "mountaineers" was approaching to reinforce Morgan. Tarleton decided to pursue Morgan, waiting for an opportunity to strike.

Morgan now faced the problem of reassembling his scattered command, and rebel couriers like young Joseph McJunkin raced about the countryside: "At this time Genl Pickens was encamped between Fairforest and Tyger to watch the movements of Tarleton and give information to Genl Morgan. I was sent as an express to Genl Morgan, Morgan then sent an express to Col Washington who was then at Wofford Iron Works to inform him of Tarleton's approach and to meet him at Gentleman Thompsons."

Thomas Young remembered that after the Hammond's Store raid the mounted force "returned to Morgan's encampment at Grindal Shoals, on the Packolette, and there we remained, eating beef and scouting through the neighborhood until we heard of Tarlton's approach. Having received intelligence that Col. Tarlton designed to cross the Packolette at Easternood Shoals above us, Gen. Morgan broke up his encampment early on the morning of the 16th, and retreated up the mountain road by Hancock's Ville, taking the left hand road not far above, in a direction toward the head of Thickety Creek. We arrived at the field of the Cowpens about sun-down, and were then told that there we should meet the enemy."

Teenaged Angelica Mitchell recalled that the Patriot rearguards "set the woods on fire, which no doubt retarded Tarleton's pursuit each time at least a fourth of an hour" although this is probably an exaggeration given the rainy weather.

By now many of the militia had a belly full of fleeing from Tarleton, and during the march there was considerable grumbling in the ranks. Thomas Young remembered that when the news spread that they would stand and fight, it was "received with great joy by the army. We were very anxious for battle, and many a hearty curse had been vented against Gen. Morgan during that day's march, for retreating, as we thought, to avoid a fight. Night came upon us, yet much remained to be done." Blackstock's had cost Tarleton much of his aura of invincibility. Local militia gathered at Hannah's Cowpens, eager to fight without being attached to any particular unit.

As always Tarleton pushed his troops and their mounts to the limits of endurance, making camp late at night and resuming the march well before dawn. His progress was slowed by the need to forage, plundering local farms. Loyalists who ranged through the countryside in Tarleton's wake made life even more miserable for local families. Angelica Mitchell remembered that Tory raiders burned her family's temporary shelter, a tent canvas stretched over a log pen filled with straw, a substitute for their home housing victims of smallpox. Winter temperatures sometimes plunged below 0°F (-18°C). "At the time Col. Tarleton came to aunt Beckham's, [the enemy] took all the bedding save one quilt. Soon afterwards a party of Tories came & took that away."

# The opponents converge, January 13–17, 1781.

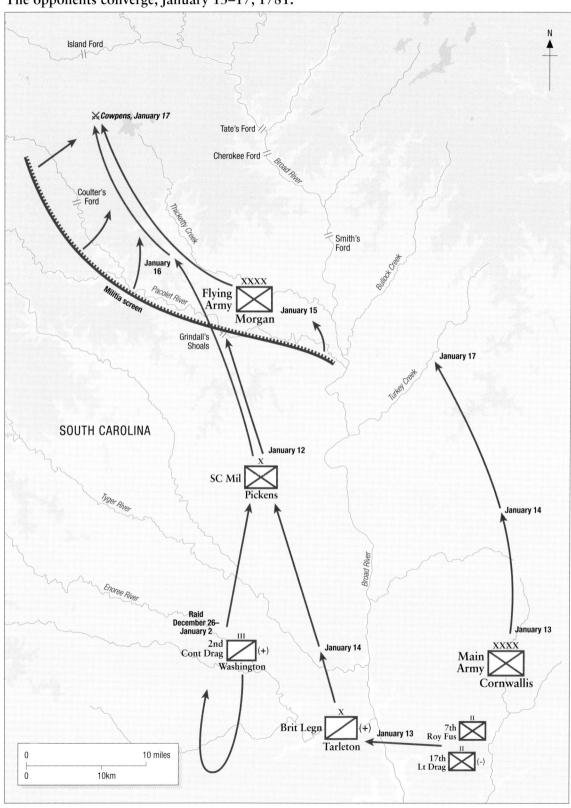

Island Ford

N

Cowpens, January 17

Tate's Ford

Cherokee Ford

Broad River

Coulter's Ford

Thicketty Creek

Smith's Ford

Bullock Creek

January 16

Militia screen

Pacolet River

Flying Army

XXXX

Morgan

January 15

Grindall's Shoals

SOUTH CAROLINA

Turkey Creek

January 17

January 14

January 12

SC Mil

X

Pickens

Tyger River

Broad River

January 13

January 14

Enoree River

Main Army

XXXX

Cornwallis

Raid December 26– January 2

2nd Cont Drag

III

(+)

Washington

January 14

Brit Legn

X

(+)

Tarleton

January 13

7th Roy Fus

II

17th Lt Drag

II

(-)

0          10 miles

0      10km

At the Cowpens orders were given to mold rifle and musket balls from 1lb (0.45kg) lead bars issued to each man. Major Samuel Hammond said that verbal orders stipulated that each man was "to have twenty-four rounds of balls prepared and ready for use, before they retired to rest. A general order, forming the disposition of the troops, in case of coming to action, had also been prepared." The men broke up into messes, small groups who cooked and ate together.

For Morgan and his senior officers, there would be little rest that night. Morgan again interviewed officers who had confronted Tarleton, and deduced that "Benny" would as usual come head-on along the Green River Road, a narrow rutted track that ran the length of the open pasture. Tarleton was a renowned cavalryman, but seldom took time to use his cavalry to probe and assess enemy positions once they were encountered. He just came on at top speed, relying upon shock to carry the day.

Morgan rode over the pastureland, examining the subtleties of the topography, what Tarleton would see as he came out of the forest. Most accounts of the battle depict the Cowpens as fairly flat, open terrain. The main militia line described the ground to their front as relatively flat, with low-growing vegetation and scattered shrubs.

The most important feature of the battlefield is far less obvious. Running across the Green River Road is a very low ridge not easily perceived, with a second small rise behind. A century later historian J. B. O. Landrum observed: "The only rising ground of any note on the whole field is a little eminence a short distance in the rear of the ridge, where the main line formed. This is of sufficient height to cover a man on horseback placed in the rear of it." Today, men positioned in the rear of the first low ridge – even with closely mown grass and an absence of shrubs – are invisible. In the swale behind the first ridge was a grove of pines whose morning shadows further concealed Morgan's troops positioned inside.

British infantry were armed primarily with the Tower (top) and Short Tower (middle) muskets. The contemporary French Charleville musket (bottom) is shown for comparison. (USMC History Division)

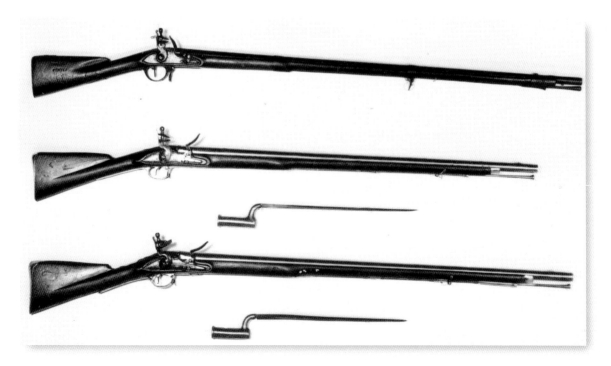

Much has been made of the fact that some described the battle site as bounded on both sides by ravines, densely wooded swamps, and nearly impenetrable canebrakes. The boggy ground and canebrakes were real enough, but the "ravines" are really gentle slopes down into adjacent streams. The inference is that the adjacent terrain would have limited flanking movements by Tarleton's dragoons. Morgan realized that he had insufficient troops for a linear defense, and during the battle dragoons from both sides rode freely around both ends of the main battle lines.

Morgan's ingenious, but risky, plan was to use the subtleties of the terrain, well-known British doctrine, and Tarleton's recklessness to his advantage.

Continuing changes of troop dispositions necessitated by the influx of local militia, and probably anxiety, kept Morgan on the move through the night. One of his primary needs was more cavalry. Most militiamen were mounted infantry but few were equipped to fight as cavalry. Morgan had extensive experience commanding militia, and knew their capabilities and limitations all too well. In a partisan war of raids and ambushes, they excelled. But in formal combat in the open field against trained infantry the militia had very limited capabilities.

In the hands of a skilled user the more accurate but slow to reload rifle used by some militiamen could fire about two rounds per minute. The rifle had a front sight bead, which made it impossible to mount a socket bayonet, and the bore was too small for a plug bayonet. Riflemen were at a terrible disadvantage in close combat against trained infantry equipped with bayonets, and were usually relegated to duty as skirmishers or placed in positions where they could be protected from close attack.

The smoothbore muskets used by the American Continentals and State Troops, British Redcoats and Provincials, and in fact most of the militia on both sides was less accurate, but prepared cartridges gave them a rate of fire of about three rounds per minute.

The Continentals, armed with French Charleville muskets, were supplied with a standardized load of 40 rounds of buck-and-ball – a .69-caliber (18mm) main ball, typically four .30-caliber (7.62mm) buckshot, and a standard powder charge, all wrapped in a paper cartridge. Four spare flints completed the infantryman's load. The sub-caliber buckshot inflicted serious wounds, and greatly increased the chances of striking flesh with at least one ball.

The typical weapon of both the British Redcoat and Loyalist Provincial infantryman was the Short Pattern Tower musket, the famous Brown Bess. This .69-caliber weapon was also provided with buck-and-ball ammunition.

A key advantage of the military musket was that it could be fitted with a socket bayonet. In the hands of British Regulars and Provincials, and American Continentals and State Troops, the bayonet was an efficient and intimidating killing tool. Few militiamen were equipped with bayonets, and almost none were trained in their use unless they had prior service as Continentals.

The primary close-combat weapons of militia were the tomahawk and knife, near-suicidal weapons when pitted against bayonets. Analysis of pension records and casualty records indicates most American deaths and wounds were inflicted by British edged weapons. A British bayonet charge almost inevitably threw militia into a panicked retreat. Such tactics had resulted in numerous victories, as at Horatio Gates' defeat at Camden.

Unlike most Continental officers, Morgan did not completely disdain the militia, but he was realistic:

I would not have had a swamp in view of my militia for any consideration. They would have made for it, and nothing could have detained them from it. As to covering my wings, I knew my adversary and was perfectly sure I should have nothing but downright fighting. As to retreat, it was the very thing I wished to cut off all hope of. I would have thanked Tarleton had he surrounded me with his cavalry. It would have been better than placing my own men in the rear to shoot down all those who broke from the ranks. When men are forced to fight, they will sell their lives dearly, and I knew that the dread of Tarleton's cavalry would give due weight to the protection of my bayonets and keep my troops from breaking as Buford's regiment did. Had I crossed the river, one-half of my militia would immediately have abandoned me.

Morgan planned that the hard core of Continentals and Virginia militia would decide the battle, but the local militia contingent was fundamental to the tactical trap Morgan devised. It was crucial that each militiaman in this peculiarly democratic army understand his role. Subordinate officers were briefed on his plan. According to Thomas Young:

He went among the volunteers, helped them fix their swords, joked with them about their sweet-hearts, told them to keep in good spirits, and the day would be ours. And long after I laid down, he was going about among the soldiers encouraging them, and telling them that the old wagoner would crack his whip over Ben, in the morning, as sure as they lived. "Just hold up your heads, boys, three fires" he would say, "and you are free, and then when you return to your homes, how the old folks will bless you, and the girls kiss you, for your gallant conduct!" I don't believe he slept a wink that night!

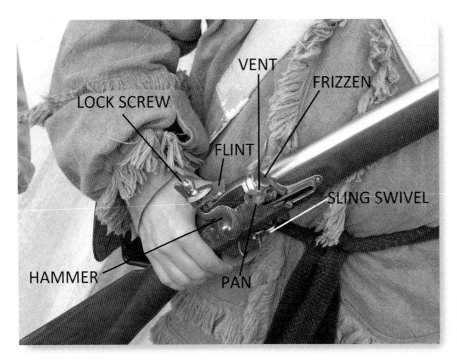

Nomenclature of a typical flintlock weapon, in this case a British Short Tower musket. (Authors' photograph)

Lieutenant Roderick MacKenzie of the 71st Foot wrote, in a critique of Tarleton's memoir, that on the British side "the detachment, by fatiguing marches, attained the ground which Morgan had quitted a few hours before: This position was taken about ten o'clock on the evening of the 16th of January." For the coming battle, Morgan's troops would be rested, well fed, and ready. Tarleton's troops would be exhausted, hungry, and sleep-deprived.

Morgan was well aware of Tarleton's penchant for dawn surprise attacks. Christopher Brandon recalled: "About daylight, I recollect Morgan's coming up to our fire, where Col. Brandon lay stretched on the ground (for we had no tents) and I well remember his morning salutation 'Get up, my fellows, – why here asleep, and the British almost in sight'. We were up in quick time and formed in order, and I'm sure there never was a set of men more anxious for battle. I was in Col. Brandon's Regiment, and marched into the line in quick time."

Tarleton did not spare his weary men or horses. Roderick MacKenzie wrote: "The pursuit re-commenced by two o'clock the next morning, and was rapidly continued through marshes and broken ground till day-light, when the enemy were discovered in front."

The history of the 7th Fusiliers has the final pursuit commencing at 3.00am. "Three light companies supported by the infantry of the Legion, formed the advance; the Royal Fusiliers, the guns, and the 71st followed; the cavalry and mounted infantry brought up the rear. It was a tedious march; for the troops had to pass over rough, broken country, much intersected by creeks and ravines; moreover, during the darkness, it was necessary to carefully examine the front and flanks, and thus a good deal of time was lost."

Tarleton believed he had Morgan trapped with his back to the deep Broad River, a significant military obstacle. (Authors' photograph)

# THE BATTLE OF COWPENS

More than the usual fog of war attends any description of the battle of Cowpens. Most accounts were written well after the event, and often by less-educated militia officers and common soldiers. This is not necessarily a great handicap in one sense; commanders often make excuses to justify their failures, and Banastre Tarleton's memoir, often considered the definitive first-person account, is a superb example. The Cowpens battle, particularly in its decisive latter phases, unfolded with such rapidity that most of the participants cannot place significant tactical events in a precise temporal sequence. In some cases first-person accounts are contradictory, simply because a soldier or officer was seeing only the chaotic events unfolding in his immediate vicinity. An example is the nearly disastrous flight of the militia on the American left flank, described very differently by several participants.

In this retelling of the battle we have drawn upon period accounts, military pension statements, our own analysis from walking the battlefield and related sites, and made judicious use of secondary analyses by various historians (most written long after the battle).

Morgan made skilful use of the subtle topography, concealing his main line behind Militia Rise, the very subtle rise that lay athwart the Green River Road. (Authors' photograph)

# MORGAN'S TACTICAL DISPOSITIONS

Morgan's tactical dispositions did not in themselves win the battle, since the latter clearly did not go as planned, but his initial planning did set the stage for what was to follow. The boundaries of the battle space were marked by a transition from the relatively open grazing area to more densely wooded areas, and in some areas to dense stands of native switch cane. Switch cane grows in dense groves on wet ground, and is penetrable only with difficulty by men on foot or horses. These changes in vegetation resulted from very minor changes in drainage. In the late 18th century writers described springs – since dried up – that kept this very slightly lower ground wet and soft, unsuitable for men on horseback.

In fleshing out the details of his plan Morgan was hampered by the last-minute influx of militiamen. Two hand-drawn maps are preserved in the US National Archives, both prepared from the memories of participants shortly after the battle, and we have examined both the undated "Clove" and February 15, 1781 "Pigree" maps. The more useful is the Clove map (the location at which the map was prepared) but the dispositions shown on the map are at odds with pension records, interviews, and other statements by the participants in the battle.

This map appears to be a graphic representation of Morgan's planned dispositions at the time he issued verbal orders late on the night of January 16. Most noticeable are that positions of Morgan's local militia units are reversed in the forward defensive line. The document is useful in that it clearly depicts Morgan's intent for a defense in depth, with pre-planned withdrawal routes and secondary fighting positions for the militia, and crude hachures that depict the position of his Continentals and the Virginia militia in a reverse-slope defense behind the low rise.

Another intriguing aspect of this map is the numbers written on it. Some clearly indicate Tarleton's troop strengths for selected units. At the bottom is a tally which we suspect represents Morgan's known troop strength at the time the plan depicted on the map was conceived, totaling 889 men. Two numbers, 80 and 170, are suspiciously close to the known strengths of Washington's dragoons and Howard's Continentals, respectively.

Rather than an orthodox linear defense, Morgan's defense was a very unusual multi-layered reverse slope defense.

Morgan's first line would be an orthodox skirmish line. This first line consisted of riflemen from Colonel Joseph "Quaker Meadows Joe" McDowell's North Carolina militia battalion and South Carolina State Troops under Major Samuel Hammond. (There were two Colonel Joseph McDowells – pronounced "McDool" – hence the nickname.) Skirmishers were a common military practice of the era, and what Tarleton would have expected.

Some of Hammond's men were hastily provided with swords from Morgan's stores, and detailed as cavalry under Captain Joseph Pickens, younger brother of the brigade commander. Those who "were not so equipped were armed with rifles" under Hammond's command.

The skirmishers were expected to "bring on the action," forcing the enemy to deploy, gaining time for the commander to assess enemy strength and dispositions while in turn preventing the enemy dragoons from feeling out the American positions, and in this case beginning an attrition process by targeting British officers and NCOs. Not trained as light infantry, Morgan's

Tall grass and scattered trees obstructed the "open plain," further concealing Morgan's positions. (Authors' photograph)

skirmishers deployed in loose clumps for mutual protection on ground that sloped gently down toward the approaching enemy. Lacking bayonets, they would fire their slow to reload rifles in rotation so that some always remained ready to fire in case of an enemy cavalry attack. The meticulous Morgan specifically instructed them to "shelter their bodies and fire from the side [of trees] ... and when charged by the enemy's cavalry, that [one should fire and] two should hold their fire in reserve."

Morgan's second line – clearly visible militia – was bait. This line was deployed on or very near the crest of the "rising ground," the very gentle forward slope of the first small ridge to the southwest (British left) of the Green River Road. Covered by scrub vegetation and morning ground fog, the rise was imperceptible from Tarleton's vantage point, and the entire militia line was probably not visible to Tarleton. South Carolina militiaman Christopher Brandon recalled that "The battle field was almost a plain, with little or no undergrowth. On our left flank was a miry branch [the head of Suck Creek], in front of which the 'Long cane' men under McCall were stationed. *A slight rise on the ground prevented our seeing the enemy, until they came within eighty yards of us* [italics added]."

Pickens' militia brigade was arrayed across the road, with four regiments from the Patriots right to left: Roebuck, Thomas, Hayes, and Brandon. Some authors have interpreted this as a traditional European right-to-left-of-line regimental seniority, but Morgan – and certainly his militia colonels – cared little for such niceties. Within each regiment expert marksmen were instructed to take up positions ahead of the main line to snipe at enemy leaders and continue the process of decapitating the British command structure.

When militia eventually broke and ran, their usual practice, it inevitably triggered a headlong pursuit that disrupted the famed British unit integrity. Morgan's plan was to have the militia hastily withdraw to secondary positions on the flanks of the main line of Continentals and Virginia militia to surprise a disorganized British charge with a waiting line of highly disciplined regulars when they topped the ridge. The low rise, vegetation, and standing militiamen

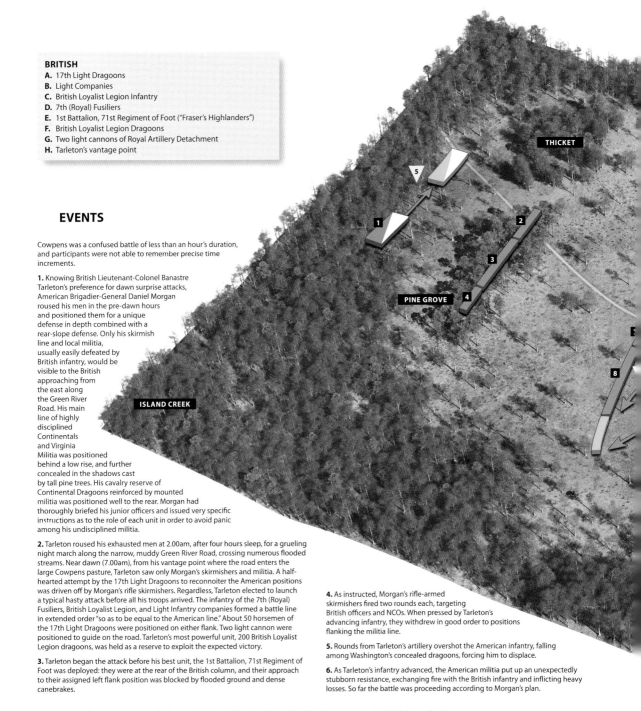

## EVENTS

Cowpens was a confused battle of less than an hour's duration, and participants were not able to remember precise time increments.

**1.** Knowing British Lieutenant-Colonel Banastre Tarleton's preference for dawn surprise attacks, American Brigadier-General Daniel Morgan roused his men in the pre-dawn hours and positioned them for a unique defense in depth combined with a rear-slope defense. Only his skirmish line and local militia, usually easily defeated by British infantry, would be visible to the British approaching from the east along the Green River Road. His main line of highly disciplined Continentals and Virginia Militia was positioned behind a low rise, and further concealed in the shadows cast by tall pine trees. His cavalry reserve of Continental Dragoons reinforced by mounted militia was positioned well to the rear. Morgan had thoroughly briefed his junior officers and issued very specific instructions as to the role of each unit in order to avoid panic among his undisciplined militia.

**2.** Tarleton roused his exhausted men at 2.00am, after four hours sleep, for a grueling night march along the narrow, muddy Green River Road, crossing numerous flooded streams. Near dawn (7.00am), from his vantage point where the road enters the large Cowpens pasture, Tarleton saw only Morgan's skirmishers and militia. A half-hearted attempt by the 17th Light Dragoons to reconnoiter the American positions was driven off by Morgan's rifle skirmishers. Regardless, Tarleton elected to launch a typical hasty attack before all his troops arrived. The infantry of the 7th (Royal) Fusiliers, British Loyalist Legion, and Light Infantry companies formed a battle line in extended order "so as to be equal to the American line." About 50 horsemen of the 17th Light Dragoons were positioned on either flank. Two light cannon were positioned to guide on the road. Tarleton's most powerful unit, 200 British Loyalist Legion dragoons, was held as a reserve to exploit the expected victory.

**3.** Tarleton began the attack before his best unit, the 1st Battalion, 71st Regiment of Foot was deployed: they were at the rear of the British column, and their approach to their assigned left flank position was blocked by flooded ground and dense canebrakes.

**4.** As instructed, Morgan's rifle-armed skirmishers fired two rounds each, targeting British officers and NCOs. When pressed by Tarleton's advancing infantry, they withdrew in good order to positions flanking the militia line.

**5.** Rounds from Tarleton's artillery overshot the American infantry, falling among Washington's concealed dragoons, forcing him to displace.

**6.** As Tarleton's infantry advanced, the American militia put up an unexpectedly stubborn resistance, exchanging fire with the British infantry and inflicting heavy losses. So far the battle was proceeding according to Morgan's plan.

# INITIAL DISPOSITIONS AND WITHDRAWAL OF THE SKIRMISH LINE

Morgan devised an unusual defense in depth combined with a rear-slope defense. An orthodox skirmish line fronted an easily visible line of militia as bait. The skirmishers were instructed to fire twice, and then fall back to positions flanking the militia line. Morgan's main line of Continentals and Virginia militia was concealed behind a low rise. Tarleton deployed hastily, his Legion Infantry and Light Infantry in open order so as to equal the flanks of the American militia line, with small detachments of the 17th Light Dragoons on either flank. The 71st Foot was not fully organized from the march, and the British Legion dragoons were held as a reserve to exploit the expected victory.

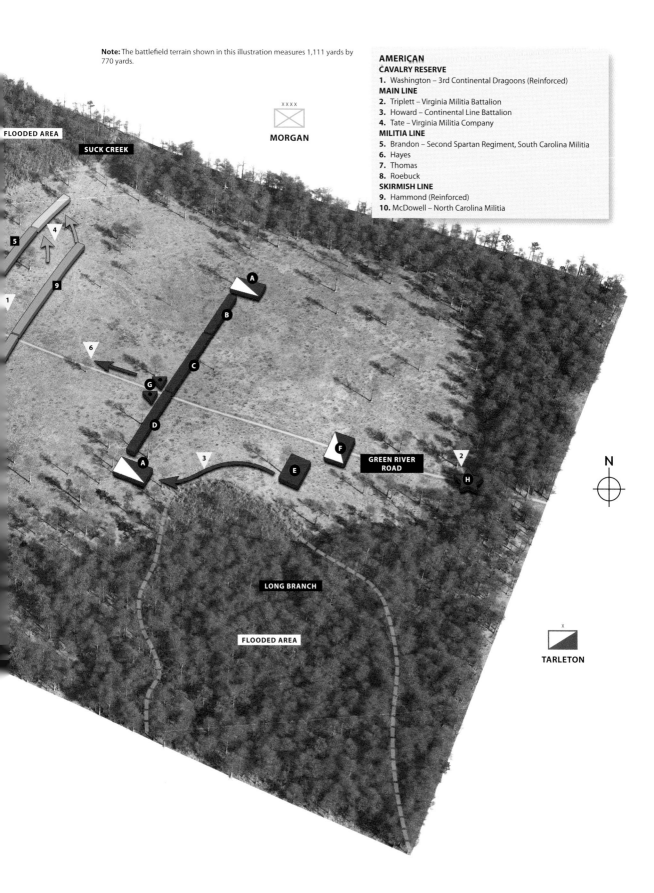

**Note:** The battlefield terrain shown in this illustration measures 1,111 yards by 770 yards.

XXXX
**MORGAN**

**AMERICAN**
**CAVALRY RESERVE**
**1.** Washington – 3rd Continental Dragoons (Reinforced)
**MAIN LINE**
**2.** Triplett – Virginia Militia Battalion
**3.** Howard – Continental Line Battalion
**4.** Tate – Virginia Militia Company
**MILITIA LINE**
**5.** Brandon – Second Spartan Regiment, South Carolina Militia
**6.** Hayes
**7.** Thomas
**8.** Roebuck
**SKIRMISH LINE**
**9.** Hammond (Reinforced)
**10.** McDowell – North Carolina Militia

FLOODED AREA

SUCK CREEK

GREEN RIVER ROAD

N

LONG BRANCH

FLOODED AREA

X
**TARLETON**

51

SCENE AT THE COWPENS.

Although the battle site was often described as an "open plain," it was more like this early 19th-century depiction. (Lossing)

effectively concealed the main line. This line was positioned in a grove of loblolly pines, and the shade of these large evergreen trees offered additional concealment in the dim morning light. (Several Continentals remembered the morning chill, unabated by the warmth of the sun.) The Continentals formed the center of the main line, with Triplett's battalion to their left and Captain James Tate's company of drafted militia to the right.

The inherent risk was that once in motion the militia would simply keep going and abandon the Continentals. This had happened on numerous prior occasions, and the Camden debacle was undoubtedly in Morgan's thoughts. The key was to motivate the militia to stand and fight, and to make sure the militia understood their role.

Scots historian David Stewart provided an insight from the British viewpoint, noting that "[Morgan's] force drawn up on a rising ground, thinly covered with pine trees; the front line being on the crown of the rising ground, and the second 400 paces in rear of the first line." Morgan counted on Tarleton to come straight up the middle, guiding on the road. A successful cavalry sweep around either American flank would have revealed the concealed American main line.

Washington's reserve force of dragoons was farther to the rear on the next rising ground, also screened by the terrain and militia line.

The history of the 7th Fusiliers recorded that, "Before dawn, Thickelle [Thicketty] Creek was passed; then an advanced guard of dragoons was sent forward, and presently fell in with an American patrol, which was pursued and overtaken. A squadron of dragoons was now ordered to reinforce the advance guard, and harass the enemy's rear, and before long the officer commanding the advance guard reported that Morgan's troops were halting and forming."

American Thomas Young recalled:

> Our pickets were stationed three miles in advance. Samuel Clowney was one of the picket guard, and I often heard him afterwards laugh at his narrow escape. Three of Washington's dragoons were out on a scout, when they came almost in contact with the advanced guard of the British army; they wheeled, and were pursued almost into camp. Two got in safely; one poor fellow, whose horse fell down, was taken prisoner. It was about day[break] that the pickets were driven in.

Lieutenant Roderick MacKenzie wrote: "Two of their videttes were taken soon after; these gave information that General Morgan had halted, and prepared for action; he had formed his troops as described by Ramsey, in an open wood, secured neither in front, flank, nor rear." Note that Mackenzie debunks the idea that Morgan anchored his flanks on ravines.

This time there would be no dawn surprise. The firing by the American pickets, messengers, and general hullabaloo gave ample warning of Tarleton's approach.

# BRITISH TACTICAL DISPOSITION

Tarleton had to deploy from an order of march imposed by the narrow forest-bounded road. When Tarleton at last viewed the American pickets and militia line, he decided to – as usual – barge right in before his force was fully deployed.

As seems usual, the period maps are contradictory in details. The initial assault would be made against Morgan's skirmishers by only part of the British in extended order, with the two artillery pieces guiding on the road. Dragoons would take up position on the flanks, with the 71st Foot and the Legion cavalry in reserve.

As infantry units arrived on the field, they grounded their marching packs and formed into battle order, but were granted no time for a brief rest. MacKenzie recalled:

> Without the delay of a single moment, and in despite of extreme fatigue, the light-legion infantry and fusileers were ordered to form in line. Before this order was put in execution, and while Major Newmarsh, who commanded the latter corps, was posting his officers, the line, far from complete, was led to the attack by Lieutenant Colonel Tarleton himself. The seventy-first regiment and [British Legion] cavalry, who had as yet not disentangled themselves from the brush-wood with which Thickelle Creek abounds, were directed to form, and wait for orders.

From the American side, Private James Collins wrote that about dawn "the enemy came in full view. The sight, to me at least, seemed somewhat imposing; they halted for a short time. We look'd at each other for a considerable time." Lieutenant Thomas Anderson from the Delaware Continentals recalled that the enemy "halted and Form'd the Line in Full View as We had no artillery to annoy them." (This would suggest that at least some of the Continentals could see past the militia line to their front.)

# BATTLE IS JOINED

As Tarleton rode into the cleared pastureland, he saw exactly the enemy dispositions he expected, the skirmishers and militia line, and that probably only dimly in the morning light and ground fog. His local informants, particularly Loyalist Alexander Chesney, had described the Cowpens as an open plain, with the deep and aptly named Broad River several miles to the rear: "the situation of the enemy was desperate in case of misfortune; an open country, and a river in their rear." For Tarleton this would have seemed a tactical gift: easily routed militia who would flee from a resolute bayonet charge, only to be trapped against the deep, freezing-cold water.

No matter that his men were hungry, weary, and sleep-deprived, and had just slogged five or so hours through darkness, mud, rain, and flooded streams. The history of the 7th Fusiliers states: "the replies he received [from local guides] giving him every reason to suppose that he had his adversary at a disadvantage, he determined to attack at once." From a common soldier's point of view the history of the 7th Fusiliers undoubtedly exaggerated: "nevertheless, they were eager to try conclusions with the enemy, and received the order to advance with enthusiasm." Tarleton instructed his men that no prisoners were to be taken.

In his memoir Tarleton sought to partially shift blame for his precipitate attack onto Cornwallis. "Lieutenant-Colonel Tarleton … did not hesitate to undertake those measures which the instructions of his commanding officer imposed, and his own judgement, under the present appearances, equally recommended. He ordered the legion dragoons to drive in the militia parties who covered the front, that General Morgan's dispositions might be conveniently and distinctly inspected." He went on at length to imply that this brief foray revealed the complete disposition of Morgan's force, an assertion contradicted by every other account, including those of the British participants.

The British dragoons could not drive the enemy skirmishers, but turned and rode parallel to the skirmish line, exposed to deadly rifle fire. Undaunted by the failure of this gambit, Tarleton deployed for battle. In the American militia line the men were standing ready, and Thomas Young recalled that at first light the day was "bitterly cold. We were formed in order of battle, and the men were slapping their hands together to keep warm—an exertion not long necessary." Militiaman Henry Connelly said that to add to the misery, "it was inclined to be raining during this battle." Private James Collins recalled that "the enemy … halted for a short time, and then advanced rapidly, as if certain of victory."

The short interval is another indication of Tarleton's haste, as was his failure to use his small artillery detachment to soften up Morgan's position. Artillery seldom played a decisive role in these battles, but Tarleton's grasshopper guns gave him a distinct advantage. The protracted fire of the small cannons, directed at the clearly visible militia, would have done much to demoralize or even break the militia before an infantry assault. Some authors have downplayed the potential efficacy of the cannons, citing a short effective range. The range of the guns was clearly not an issue: of the limited number of rounds fired, several went over the heads of the militia and Continentals to fall among Washington's dragoons far to the rear, forcing them to displace.

Tarleton described his hasty deployment, as usual referring to himself in the third person:

Locally made, low-quality black powder produced dense clouds of smoke, far worse than that produced by modern powder used by these militia re-enactors. This smoke further obscured vision on the battlefield and made tactical control difficult. Note the historically accurate mix of rifles (powder horns) and muskets (slings and cartouches). (Authors' photograph)

He desired his infantry to disencumber themselves of everything, except their arms and ammunition. The light infantry were then ordered to file to the right till they became equal to the flank of the American front line; The Legion infantry were added to their left; and, under the fire of a three-pounder, this part of the British troops was instructed to advance within three-hundred yards of the enemy. This situation being acquired, the 7th Regiment was commanded to form upon the left of the Legion infantry, and the other three-pounder was given to the right division of the 7th; A captain with fifty dragoons was placed on each flank of the corps, who formed the British front line, to protect their own, and threaten the flanks of the enemy: The 1st battalion of the 71st was desired to extend a little to the left of the 7th Regiment, and to remain one hundred and fifty yards in the rear. This body of infantry, and near two hundred cavalry, composed the reserve. During the execution of these arrangements, the animation of the officers, and the alacrity of the soldiers, afforded the most promising assurances of success.

The American skirmishers gave ground grudgingly as the British infantry advanced. When the attack commenced, the 71st Foot was still not deployed in its reserve position, and the favored Green Dragoons were being held as a reserve to charge when the American militia broke and ran.

Inexplicably, Colonel Joseph Hayes' Little River Regiment advanced toward the British, opening a gap in the militia line, then just as suddenly moved backward to close the gap, so no harm was done.

The British infantry advanced confidently at the quick step. The American skirmishers had orders to hold fire until the enemy closed within 50 yards (45m), fire twice, then withdraw toward the flanks of the militia line.

Private Joseph McJunkin recalled Morgan's efforts to steady his militia line, walking behind and shouting, "Boys, squinney [squint] well and don't fire until you see the whites of their eyes."

Private Thomas Young could also clearly hear Morgan's booming voice. He recalled that "the British line advanced at a sort of trot, with a loud halloo. It was the most beautiful line I ever saw. When they shouted, I heard Morgan say, 'They give us the British halloo, boys, give them the Indian halloo, by G—;' and he galloped along the lines, cheering the men, and telling them not to fire until we could see the whites of their eyes. Every officer was crying don't fire! for it was a hard matter for us to keep from it. I should have said the British line advanced under cover of their artillery; for it opened so fiercely upon the center, that Col. Washington moved his cavalry."

Thomas Young recalled: "The militia fired first. It was for a time, pop—pop—pop—and then a whole volley … I have heard old Col. Fair [Farr] say often, that he believed John Savage fired the first gun in this battle. He was riding to and fro, along the lines, when he saw Savage fix his eye upon a British officer." The officer rode toward the militia line and "calling them in a loud voice 'Dam'd Rebels' and ordered them to disperse – John Savage instantly raised his rifle and the British officer fell [from] his horse mortally wounded."

The British right closed with the militia line first, and the militia fired the first volley. Inexplicably, the Second Spartans got off a second volley, stopping the Light Infantry in their tracks as firing spread along the lines. Christopher Brandon stated: "With a shout they came on in a beautiful line, and a solid flame of fire burst from one end to the other. Our orders were for only one

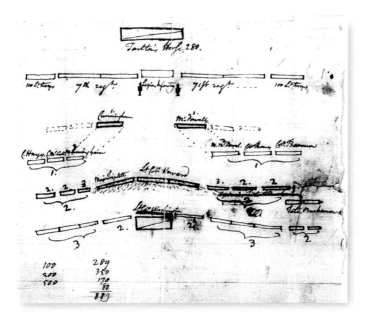

Several contradictory contemporary maps of the battle survive, like the so-called "Pigree map." The numbers at lower left seem to be a tally of troop strengths, and the small dashes indicate the small rise. (Library of Congress)

third to fire at a time, but the anxiety of the men was so great, that many of them broke ranks, and rushing forward, jumped behind trees, and commenced the fight on their own responsibility."

On the British side the punishment from the American fire caused a rare and noteworthy breakdown in discipline: "the Royal Fusiliers advanced, with the rest of the front line, and in this advance their recruits opened fire too soon; their fire was, however, quickly suppressed." Tarleton recorded that "the troops moved on in as good a line as troops could move *at open files* [italics added]."

Scots historian David Stewart recorded that the American militia, against all precedent, stood their ground against the Redcoats:

Exhausted by running, [the British line] received the fire of the enemy at the distance of thirty or forty paces. The effect of the fire was considerable: it produced something like a recoil, but not to any extent. The fire was returned, but not with vivacity or impression; and it continued ten or twelve minutes in a state of balance, both parties keeping their ground. The Light infantry made two attempts to charge, but were repulsed with loss. The action making no progress, the Highlanders were ordered up.

In his memoir Tarleton would disparage the 7th Fusiliers, but American sources attributed heavy fighting to this sector, and described the sight of British soldiers lying dead in ranks. The Light Infantry on the British right had taken a terrible mauling. Whatever the reason, the fighting had been unexpectedly intense at the militia line. MacKenzie recalled: "A number, not less than two-thirds of the British infantry officers, had already fallen, and nearly the same proportion of privates." Casualties and unexpectedly heavy resistance forced the British infantry line to close to the left, shortening their line.

On the whole, Tarleton's description of the battle is unusually straightforward. MacKenzie's account differs slightly in the timing of actions from American and other British accounts: "The reserve [71st Foot and Legion Dragoons], which as yet had no orders to move from its first position, and consequently remained near a mile distant [actually about a quarter of that distance – 1,200ft/365m], was now directed to advance." The 71st had already been taking casualties inflicted by rounds that overshot the infantry line.

As the exchange of fire continued, the 71st moved forward into the confined space between the left of the British line and the nearby woods and boggy ground at the head of Long Branch, probably at the double-quick. Their right collided with the left of the 7th Fusiliers. The congestion threw both units into momentary confusion. In his memoir Tarleton wrote that he had foreseen this, and that the 71st had been specifically "directed not to entangle their right flank with the left of the other battalion." Whether

Tarleton had actually given this order is problematical. MacKenzie did not attribute significant confusion to this, but the collision caused at least some confusion, and may have contributed to what happened next.

Once the tangle was resolved, the British infantry line resumed its forward motion. In Tarleton's words, "The continentals and backwoodsmen gave ground: The British rushed forwards: An order was dispatched to the cavalry to charge." In reality there were no Continentals in the American first line, and MacKenzie said that the British infantry "was not to be resisted by an American militia. They gave way on all quarters, and were pursued to their continentals."

The militia's planned but sudden withdrawal caught the British infantry off balance. Even decades later, some British historians insisted that the militia retreated in "confusion." Morgan's plan, as depicted in period sketch maps, was for the militia to withdraw to positions flanking the Continentals, but the militia line was quite long. Some militiamen from the center would have to move a considerable distance across the front of the Continentals, potentially masking their fire.

In the heat of battle the withdrawal of the militia did not go nearly as well as Morgan had hoped. In the center militiamen of Hayes' and Thomas' commands were able to execute a fairly orderly withdrawal, aided by the discipline of the Continentals, who opened a gap in their line to allow withdrawal. The maneuver particularly impressed the Scots historian Stewart: "the Highlanders were ordered up; and, rapidly advancing in charge, the enemy's front line moved off precipitately; and the second, which had as yet taken no share in the action, observing confusion and retrograding in their front, suddenly faced to the right, and inclined backwards; a manoeuvre by which a space was left for the front line to retreat, without interfering with the ranks of those who were now to oppose the advance of the Highlanders." Stewart was writing four decades later, with the benefit of access to American accounts. It should be noted that the British almost certainly did not actually see this maneuver, since they had not yet crested the low rise, and therefore had not yet encountered Morgan's line of Continentals waiting in the shadows on the rear slope. The militia who passed through this gap would have been easily corralled and re-formed by Morgan's aides.

Precisely as Morgan had feared, much of McDowell's command on the American extreme right made for nearby boggy woods. The confusion on Morgan's right was exacerbated when Tarleton's dragoons charged in to turn the American right flank in pursuit of the retreating militiamen. MacKenzie noted: "Captain Ogilvie, with his troops [part of the 17th Dragoons], which did not exceed forty men, was ordered to charge the right flank of the enemy. He cut his way through their line." The melee between McDowell's men and the dragoons delayed the cavalry by a few minutes, which would prove crucial.

Simultaneously, on the American left, Brandon and Hammond's commands were in a far more perilous position. Some researchers have suggested that Brandon's sizeable command also withdrew through the line of Continentals, but pension statements indicate otherwise. To move directly into their designated position to the left of the Continentals they would have to withdraw farther, across flatter, drier, open ground more suitable to cavalry action.

The two commands successfully disengaged from the British Light Infantry, but Roderick MacKenzie attributed the failure of any immediate organized infantry pursuit to Tarleton's relentless drive: "The infantry was

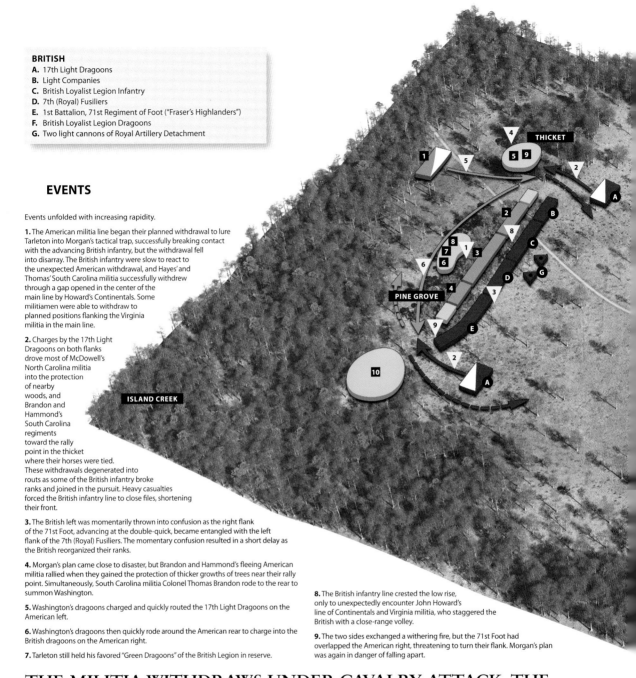

**BRITISH**
A. 17th Light Dragoons
B. Light Companies
C. British Loyalist Legion Infantry
D. 7th (Royal) Fusiliers
E. 1st Battalion, 71st Regiment of Foot ("Fraser's Highlanders")
F. British Loyalist Legion Dragoons
G. Two light cannons of Royal Artillery Detachment

## EVENTS

Events unfolded with increasing rapidity.

**1.** The American militia line began their planned withdrawal to lure Tarleton into Morgan's tactical trap, successfully breaking contact with the advancing British infantry, but the withdrawal fell into disarray. The British infantry were slow to react to the unexpected American withdrawal, and Hayes' and Thomas' South Carolina militia successfully withdrew through a gap opened in the center of the main line by Howard's Continentals. Some militiamen were able to withdraw to planned positions flanking the Virginia militia in the main line.

**2.** Charges by the 17th Light Dragoons on both flanks drove most of McDowell's North Carolina militia into the protection of nearby woods, and Brandon and Hammond's South Carolina regiments toward the rally point in the thicket where their horses were tied. These withdrawals degenerated into routs as some of the British infantry broke ranks and joined in the pursuit. Heavy casualties forced the British infantry line to close files, shortening their front.

**3.** The British left was momentarily thrown into confusion as the right flank of the 71st Foot, advancing at the double-quick, became entangled with the left flank of the 7th (Royal) Fusiliers. The momentary confusion resulted in a short delay as the British reorganized their ranks.

**4.** Morgan's plan came close to disaster, but Brandon and Hammond's fleeing American militia rallied when they gained the protection of thicker growths of trees near their rally point. Simultaneously, South Carolina militia Colonel Thomas Brandon rode to the rear to summon Washington.

**5.** Washington's dragoons charged and quickly routed the 17th Light Dragoons on the American left.

**6.** Washington's dragoons then quickly rode around the American rear to charge into the British dragoons on the American right.

**7.** Tarleton still held his favored "Green Dragoons" of the British Legion in reserve.

**8.** The British infantry line crested the low rise, only to unexpectedly encounter John Howard's line of Continentals and Virginia militia, who staggered the British with a close-range volley.

**9.** The two sides exchanged a withering fire, but the 71st Foot had overlapped the American right, threatening to turn their flank. Morgan's plan was again in danger of falling apart.

# THE MILITIA WITHDRAWS UNDER CAVALRY ATTACK, THE AMERICAN MAIN LINE IS ENGAGED

The American militia exchanged fire with the British infantry for longer than expected. They then began a planned withdrawal to lure Tarleton into Morgan's trap, but the withdrawal fell into disarray. Some militia withdrew through a gap opened in the center of the main line, and others successfully withdrew to positions flanking the Virginia militia. Charges by the 17th Light Dragoons on both flanks drove most of McDowell's militia into a nearby swamp, and Brandon and Hammond's commands toward a rally point where their horses were tied. Militia resistance stiffened, and a counter-charge by Washington's dragoons drove off the 17th, first on the American left, then on the right. The British infantry closed files to narrow its front and the 71st Foot came on line, only to unexpectedly encounter the American main line as they crested the low rise. A brutal exchange of fire between the opposing infantry ensued, but the 71st was in position to outflank the American right.

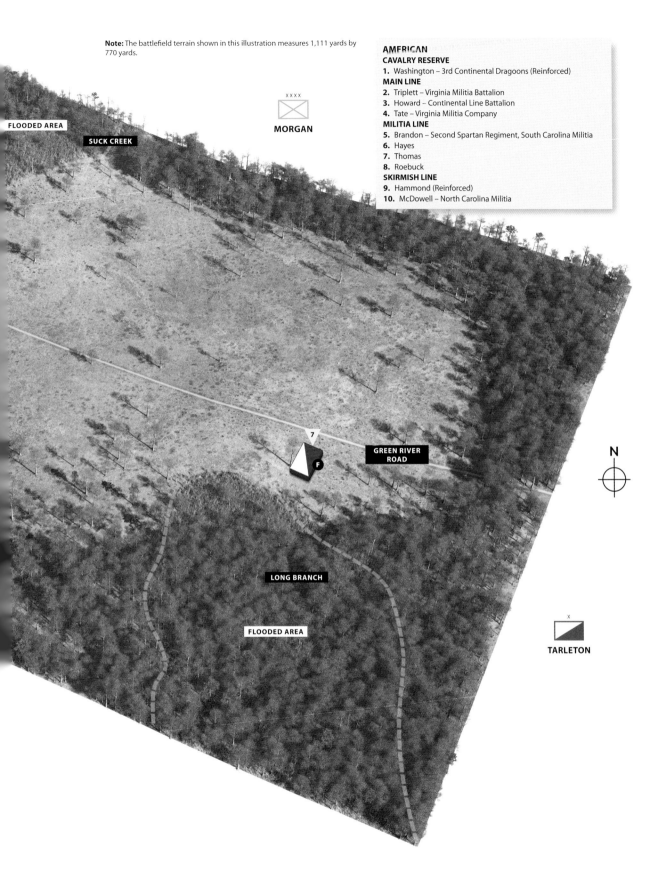

**Note:** The battlefield terrain shown in this illustration measures 1,111 yards by 770 yards.

FLOODED AREA

SUCK CREEK

xxxx

MORGAN

**AMERICAN**

**CAVALRY RESERVE**
1. Washington – 3rd Continental Dragoons (Reinforced)

**MAIN LINE**
2. Triplett – Virginia Militia Battalion
3. Howard – Continental Line Battalion
4. Tate – Virginia Militia Company

**MILITIA LINE**
5. Brandon – Second Spartan Regiment, South Carolina Militia
6. Hayes
7. Thomas
8. Roebuck

**SKIRMISH LINE**
9. Hammond (Reinforced)
10. McDowell – North Carolina Militia

7

F

GREEN RIVER ROAD

N

LONG BRANCH

FLOODED AREA

x

TARLETON

There is surprisingly little artwork depicting Cowpens. The core of Morgan's defense was the Maryland and Delaware Continentals, depicted here in action at Guilford Courthouse (March 1781) by Charles McBarron. (US Army Historical Center)

not in condition to undertake the fugitives; the latter had not marched thirty miles in the course of the last fortnight; the former, during that time, had been in motion day and night. A number, not less than two-thirds of the British infantry officers, had already fallen, and nearly the same proportion of privates; fatigue, however, enfeebled the pursuit, much more than loss of blood." MacKenzie believed the delay afforded Morgan the opportunity to reorganize his militia. The 17th Light Dragoons' moment had now arrived, and they charged in pursuit.

An orderly withdrawal in the face of cavalry pursuit was beyond the capabilities of the militia, and they ran, with some of the British light infantry joining the chase.

This was the first of two points at which Morgan's plan came closest to disaster.

Christopher Brandon was one of those who recalled an initial, fairly orderly withdrawal on the American left: "The violent shock from the British, drove us back an hundred yards, but, loading as we went, we wheeled, and opened up a fire so destructive, that the British recoiled, and we pressed forward until we were on the high ground with the Regulars again – who, brave fellows, had maintained their position."

Most of the militiamen on the left flank recalled a far graver situation. Many kept going to the position where their horses were tied, as Henry Connelly recalled "about four hundred paces in the rear."

Those most at risk were the men of Joseph Hughes' company from Brandon's regiment. Posted to the regiment's far right, they had the greatest distance to traverse across the Continentals' front. Inevitably, the enemy dragoons overtook the militiamen. The flint fell out of Hughes's rifle and "he was attacked by a couple of British dragoons; he seized a small sapling, and with this defended his head from the strokes of one, and with his rifle warded off the blows of the other. One of the Savages, a comrade from his neighborhood, ran to his assistance, and having shot one of the Dragoons, Hughes clubbed his rifle and soon dispatched the other." Hughes received a severe gash on the hand. Christopher "Kit" Brandon recalled:

> Hughes could run faster than any man I ever knew. He was also a man of great personal strength. As the company to which Hughes belonged fled, pursued by Tarleton's cavalry, Hughes with drawn sword would pass them, face about and order them to stand and often struck at them with his sword to make

them halt. He called to them in a loud voice, and said: 'You damned cowards, stand and fight; there is more danger in running than fighting, and if you don't stop and fight we will all be killed.' But they continued to run by him in the utmost confusion. He would again pursue them, pass them, his speed of foot being so much greater than theirs – face about – meet them and again order them to halt. He at last succeeded.

William Washington advised Morgan "They're coming on like a mob" before Tarleton's disorganized infantry crashed into the formed and waiting Continentals and Virginia militia. (Charles McBarron, National Park Service)

Another account is more graphic: "Hughes looked like a mad bull in the time of the battle of Cowpens. He was large, strong and active, and would be ahead; he sweated and foamed at the mouth."

James Collins noted: "Tarleton's cavalry pursued us; ('now', thought I, 'my hide is in the loft') just as we got to our horses, they overtook us and began to make a few hacks at some, however, without doing much injury." Kit Brandon went on to say: "The company halted on the brow of the slope, some distance from the battle line, behind a clump of young pines that partially hid them from the cavalry of Tarleton. Others joined them instantly for self protection against the charge of the cavalry. Their guns were instantly loaded. Morgan galloped up and spoke words of encouragement – in a moment the British cavalry were at them – they delivered a deadly fire at only ten paces distance; many saddles were emptied, and the cavalry recoiled at the unexpected assault." It must have seemed that there were several Daniel Morgans on the field that day. He was everywhere: steadying the as yet unengaged Continentals who were taking fire that overshot the militia, directing Washington's dragoons, and trying to control the disorganized militia.

Colonel Thomas Brandon's men were under the immediate command of Lieutenant-Colonel William Farr (some researchers have incorrectly identified it as Farr's regiment), but a sizeable contingent were with Washington's dragoons. Brandon was mounted, and made a mad dash to the rear to summon Washington. Kit Brandon stated: "in a few moments Col. Washington's cavalry was amongst them, like a whirlwind, and the poor fellows began to keel from their horses, without being able to remount. The shock was so sudden and violent, they could not stand it, and immediately betook themselves to flight; there was no time to rally, and they appeared to be as hard to stop as a drove of wild Choctaw steers, going to a Pennsylvania market. In a few moments the clashing of swords was out of hearing and quickly out of sight."

Thomas Young joined in the fray: "just as the charge was made upon Tarleton's cavalry, I fell in with Col. Brandon who accompanied Washington in the charge. I was just about engaging a British dragoon, when Col. Brandon darted between us & killed him, & told me to follow him. We charged through the British cavalry till they left the ground."

**THE BRITISH 17TH LIGHT DRAGOONS ON THE BRITISH RIGHT (AMERICAN LEFT) FLANK ATTACK THE MILITIA (PP. 62–63)**

Morgan counted upon the withdrawal of his militia (**1**) to trigger a premature British charge. On the British right the 17th Light Dragoons (**2**) overtook the American militia, and the withdrawal devolved into a rout. Militiamen like James Collins thought "my hide is in the loft," but junior officers succeeded in turning the militia to resist just as Washington's dragoons arrived to drive off the British dragoons.

While the near rout of the militia was playing out, the British infantry had resumed some semblance of order, closed files to shorten their front, and were following the "fleeing" militia over the low rise. Despite exhaustion and unexpectedly heavy casualties, the British infantry scented victory.

The Continentals had not yet been engaged, but their position exposed them to fire that overshot the militia line. Morgan had moved back among the main line to steady the men, and Private Henry Wells of the Delaware Company recalled that "the powerful & trumpet like voice of our Commander drove fear from every bosom, and gave new energies to every arm."

The sight of disciplined Continentals was undoubtedly a shock to the British infantry. They paused briefly to dress ranks under a galling fire from American riflemen who covered the withdrawal of the last militiamen. Casualties had greatly shortened the front of the Legion infantry and Fusiliers, and the 71st was still not fully on line.

Not all of McDowell's militia had fled into the swamp. Private Richard C. Swearingen of Pilcher's Company observed that "he was one of the first Company who first fired at which time the Regulars came up and began to Poak [pour?] it into them nicely." As the Continentals fired in disciplined rotation, "it seemed like one sheet of flame from right to left." The fighting along the main line was developing into the sort of point-blank slugfest at which the Redcoats excelled, but the Americans showed no signs of giving way. Tarleton recorded: "The contest between the British infantry in the front line and the continentals seemed equally balanced, neither retreating." One American later said that the savage, stubborn exchange lasted "near thirty minutes," but the expenditure of ammunition (several veterans recalled counting their ammunition) suggests about ten minutes at most.

On the American side the Delaware Company, facing the Fusiliers that Tarleton maligned, as well as one of the British cannons, was the most badly injured, suffering about one-quarter of its strength in casualties.

The 71st Foot moved into position on the British left, screened by dragoons who had "cut their way through" McDowell's North Carolina militia, while the infantry lines flailed away at each other. Some of the 71st Foot broke away to pursue militia who had fled toward the nearby swamp. The butchery of fleeing infantry was a dragoon specialty, and they set to it with a vengeance, hacking at the virtually defenseless militiamen. Typical of the ghastly wounds of those that survived was Private Joseph James, who was "charged on by a British Dragoon and struck on the head with his sword and left on the ground for dead … that his ribs were broken loose from his back as he supposes by the horse of the Dragoon aforesaid." Private James Patterson of the Rutherford County militia was more fortunate "cut down but afterward recovered and joined the regular troops under Col. Howard and assisted during the rest of the battle."

The British infantry bayoneted the wounded as they followed in the wake of the dragoons. Most of the militia made it into the shelter of the swamp, and continued to snipe at the left flank of the 71st Foot. The right flank of the 71st Foot, facing the highest point of the low rise, advanced at a run.

The unintended effect of this attack was to extend the 71st Foot's line well beyond the American right, and this was another critical point at which Morgan's plan might have fallen apart. British dragoons were charging into the American right flank, and worse, the extended front of the 71st Foot threatened to turn the right flank of the American main line. Howard wrote

## THE COUNTERATTACK OF THE AMERICAN MILITIA AND CONTINENTAL DRAGOONS ON THE AMERICAN RIGHT (BRITISH LEFT) FLANK (PP. 66–67)

The unplanned withdrawal of John Eager Howard's Continentals and disciplined Virginia militia drew Tarleton's infantry (**1**) into a disorganized pursuit. Howard's line (**2**) suddenly turned and delivered a withering point-blank volley, then counterattacked with the bayonet. Washington's dragoons (**3**) rode around the British left and attacked the 71st Foot from the rear. Against all expectations the American militia footmen reappeared and turned both British flanks. Most of Tarleton's infantry, exhausted by days of marching, trapped and demoralized, surrendered.

that "I had but about 350 men and the british about 800, that their line extended much further than mine particularly on my right, where they were pressing forward to gain my flank." The noise and the sight of McArthur's men rushing into the attack heartened the Light Infantry and Fusiliers.

The textbook remedy was for Howard to refuse his flank, in this case to fold the unit on the American extreme right, Captain Andrew Wallace's company of Virginians, back at a right angle to present a firing front to the flanking enemy. "Whether my orders were not well understood or whether it proceeded from any other cause, in attempting this movement some disorder ensued in this company which rather fell back than faced as I wished them." Wallace was later killed, and no one will ever know the truth of the misunderstood order. (Howard unkindly attributed Wallace's behavior to the distraction of a relationship he had formed with "a vile woman of the camp.")

The situation was compounded by a withering volley from the 71st Foot. Rather than Wallace's company pivoting clockwise about a fixed left flank, the company about-faced and began to march to the rear. To Wallace's left the Virginia State Troops were struck by the same volley, and Captain John Lawson killed. In the mayhem this company also about-faced and began to withdraw. The confusion spread progressively along the line, and the Delaware Continentals fired a volley before withdrawing. The result of the confusion progressively spreading to the left along the line was a unique maneuver. The entire American main line withdrew, and wheeled clockwise as it moved to the rear.

Morgan rode up and confronted Howard about the unauthorized movement, fearing a looming disaster. Howard recalled: "I soon removed his fears by pointing to the line, and observing that men were not beaten who retreated in that order." The ever-decisive Morgan recovered quickly, and "pointing to the rising ground in the rear of the hollow way, informed him that was the ground which he wished him to occupy, and to face about."

The weary British infantry seem to have again been caught off balance by the sudden withdrawal, granting the Americans a few crucial minutes. Morgan used the brief respite to steady his infantry, riding along the back of the line, marking positions, and observing that the British pursuit was tardy.

No contemporary artwork exists, and the battle was greatly romanticized as in this 1856 depiction. Note the American uniforms from the War of 1812, and the British grenadier helmets, among other errors. (*Ballou's Pictorial*)

The British completely misunderstood what was occurring, thought the Americans broken, and eventually charged. A significant effect of the American pivot was that the 71st Foot was forced to charge on a right oblique, inadvertently shortening their line: they were no longer in a position to flank the American right.

The history of the 7th Fusiliers was typical: "The American infantry and backwoodsmen gave way, and were pursued by the exultant British, who thought the day won." The apparent opportunity for pursuit, and heavy losses among leaders, completely broke what remained of British unit cohesion. The British infantry line, including the 71st Foot on the left flank, broke into a disorganized headlong footrace. The British rush began with the 71st, and spread spontaneously along the line.

While all this was occurring, Washington had re-formed his dragoons in the American rear. He now charged and drove off the British dragoons on the 71st Foot's left, who had been delayed by the pursuit of McDowell's men into the swamp. Washington's pursuit of the retiring enemy carried him into a vantage point where he could directly observe the British infantry from deep in their flank. His dragoons turned and rode just as quickly back to the American rear. Washington hastily dispatched a message to Howard: "They're coming on like a mob. Give them one fire and I'll charge them."

The American main line fell back in good order, reloading as they moved. At that propitious moment the reassembled militia appeared above the second rise, coming to the aid of the Continentals. "Face about, give them one fire and the victory is ours," shouted Morgan as he rode along the retreating infantry line.

Howard stated: "As soon as the word was given to halt and face about the line was perfectly formed in a moment. The enemy pressed upon us in rather disorder, expecting the fate of the day was decided. They were by this time within 30 yards of us … my men with uncommon coolness gave them an unexpected and deadly fire." The history of the Fusiliers recorded: "At that moment, the retreating Americans faced about and opened so hot a fire, that the British were checked, and then thrown into confusion." The 71st Foot was coming on at a run when struck by the devastating volley. The effect on the charging British infantry was stunning.

Many veterans thought the infantry battle lasted "all day," but the infantry exchange was likely over in minutes. Sixteen-year-old conscript Private Jeremiah Preston in Triplett's command only "fired 17 rounds" in the entire battle.

Instantly seizing upon the visible enemy confusion, Howard ordered a bayonet charge into the British herd.

Militiaman James Collins recalled: "by this time both lines of the infantry were warmly engaged and we being

Johnny Shumate's painting more correctly depicts Continentals capturing Tarleton's artillery, defended by their Royal Artillery crews in blue coats, at center. (Bonk)

relieved from the pursuit of the enemy began to rally and prepare to redeem our credit, when Morgan rode up in front, and waving his sword, cried out 'Form, form, my brave fellows! Give them one more fire and the day is ours. Old Morgan was never beaten.' We then advanced briskly, and gained the right flank of the enemy."

The American militia were now "coming on like a mob," but it was a motivated and vengeful mob hell-bent on destroying Tarleton. The tactical situation was suddenly reversed. The militia on foot charged in the wake of the line infantry and more boiled around both flanks of the British infantry line.

Roderick MacKenzie recalled: "In disorder from the pursuit, unsupported by the cavalry, deprived of the assistance of the cannon, which in defiance of the utmost exertions of those who had them in charge, were now left behind, the advance of the British fell back, and communicated a panick to others, which soon became general: a total rout ensued."

Tarleton recorded: "An unexpected fire at this instant from the Americans, who came about as they were retreating, stopped the British and threw them into confusion. Exertions to make them advance were useless. The part of the cavalry which had not been engaged fell likewise into confusion, and an unaccountable panic extended itself along the whole line. The Americans, who before thought they had lost the action, taking advantage of the present situation, advanced upon the British troops, and augmented their astonishment. A general flight ensued."

The problem was that there was no place to fly to. Washington sent his dragoons sweeping around the British left and into the flank and rear of the 71st Foot, joined by McDowell's North Carolina militiamen who re-emerged from the swamp. The situation was a strange amalgam of a classic double envelopment, and a typical frontier battle of encirclement and annihilation.

Most of the veteran Redcoats – bone-tired, devastated by massive point-blank fire, and surrounded – began to throw down their arms in surrender. Others simply lay down in the tall grass. Militiaman James Collins: "they being hard-pressed in front, by Howard, and falling fast, could not stand it long. They began to throw down their arms, and surrender themselves as prisoners of war."

Tarleton recalled: "Tarleton sent directions to his cavalry to form about four hundred yards to the right of the enemy, in order to check them, whilst he endeavoured to rally the infantry to protect the guns. The [Legion] cavalry did not comply with the order, and the effort to collect the infantry was ineffectual; Neither promises nor threats could gain their attention; they surrendered or dispersed, and abandoned the guns to the artillery men, who defended them for some time with exemplary resolution."

The Continentals had forced the British infantry back in disarray, exposing the artillery that had continued to press forward, and Howard ordered his officers to rush the cannons. Captain Richard Anderson of the First Maryland Company "saw the man at one of them about to put the match to it, leveled at them. At this critical moment he ran up, and, with the assistance of his spontoon, made a spring, and lit immediately upon the gun, and spontooned the man with the match." (A spontoon was a small spear, used by officers and NCOs either as a weapon or held horizontally as a push-bar to align men in the ranks.)

Howard saw some of his men about to attack a man on the other gun "who appeared to make it a point of honor not to surrender his match. The men, provoked by his obstinacy, would have bayonetted him on the spot, had I not interfered, and desired them to spare the life of so brave a man."

The history of the 7th Fusiliers was more explicit: "[The] cavalry of the Legion had quitted the field, with the exception of some twenty men, who joined a small party of the 17th Light Dragoons. With this handful of men, Tarleton made a desperate charge."

Tarleton's personal bravery was never in question. Though generally critical of his former commander, MacKenzie wrote that "Even at this late stage of the defeat, Lieutenant Colonel Tarleton, with no more than fifty horse, hesitated not to charge the whole of Washington's cavalry, though supported by the continentals; it was a small body of officers, and a detachment of the seventeenth regiment of dragoons, who presented themselves on this desperate occasion; the loss sustained was in proportion to the danger of the enterprise, and the whole body was repulsed." In the melee one of Washington's dragoons, Samuel Cowls, knocked the saber from the hand of a British dragoon and was about to cut him down, but "The trooper gave him the Masonic sign of distress, and he spared his life."

The British dragoons fled, with a handful of officers bringing up the rear. Washington overtook them, and personally confronted Tarleton and two officers. Washington slashed at one of the officers and his sword blade snapped off in his hand. The officer was about to slash at Washington when Washington's black camp servant, sometimes referred to as Gillie, shot the man, saving Washington. Washington's sergeant-major wounded the other officer, and Tarleton fired at Washington but instead struck his horse. The British officers were able to make good an escape. This minor clash of cavalry was romanticized in numerous works of art, but was in fact irrelevant. The battle was long since decided.

The survivors of the 71st withdrew to where the American militia line had once been positioned and tried to make a stand, but the Continentals pursued too closely. Howard "called to them to surrender, they laid down their arms, and the officers delivered up their swords. Captain Duncanson, of the 71st grenadiers, gave up his sword, and stood by me. Upon getting on my horse, I found him pulling at my saddle, and he nearly unhorsed me." Howard found that the "explanation was that they had orders to give no quarter, and they did not expect any."

The best depiction of the bedraggled Continentals as they would have appeared at Cowpens is *The Old Line at Guilford Courthouse*. The same units participated in both battles. (Bryant White, www. whitehistoricart.com)

The only British troops not caught in the sack were the dragoons and some infantry stragglers. On the American left Brandon's and Hayes' men, and some of the Virginia militia, crowded in on the British, who began to surrender en masse. Thomas Young said that "The British broke, and throwing down their guns and cartouche boxes, made for the wagon road, and did the prettiest sort of running," pursued by mounted militia.

The British infantry were, in MacKenzie's words, "easily overtaken, as the cause which had retarded the pursuit, had now an equal effect in impeding the retreat: dispirited on many accounts, they surrendered at discretion."

The situation was still uncertain for the British survivors. Many of the American militiamen, whose families had suffered under Tarleton's depredations, were shouting "Tarleton's quarter!" and "Give them Buford's play!", but on neither side was there any mention of the murder of prisoners.

The surviving British dragoons fled at top speed, the Legion dragoons leading the way. George Hanger wrote that "some officers went so far as to cut down several of their men, in order to stop the flight." MacKenzie recalled: "Two hundred and fifty horse which had not been engaged, fled through the woods with utmost precipitation, bearing down such officers as opposed their flight."

Tarleton followed them back down the Green River Road. "Another party of the Americans, who had seized upon the baggage of the British troops on the road from the late encampment, were dispersed, and this detachment retired towards Broad River unmolested." The men cut down by the fleeing dragoons were actually Loyalist militiamen. Tarleton again bamboozled his commander, and Cornwallis wrote Sir Henry Clinton that "Lieutenant Colonel Tarleton retook the baggage of the corps, and cut to pieces the detachment of the enemy who had taken possession of it; and after destroying what they could not conveniently bring off, retired with the remainder, unmolested."

In fact the fleeing British were greatly "molested." A detachment, under a Lieutenant Fraser of the 71st Foot, was left to guard part of the train, and according to MacKenzie "what part of the baggage could not be carried off he immediately destroyed, and with his men mounted on the wagon, and spare horses, he retreated to Earl Cornwallis … This was the only body of infantry that escaped, the rest were either killed or made prisoner."

Militiaman James Collins said candidly: "After the fight was over, the sight was truly melancholy. The dead on the side of the British, exceeded the number killed at King's Mountain, being if I recollect, three hundred, or upwards … This day, I fired my little rifle five times, whether with any effect or not I do not know."

Through the remainder of the day and into the night American mounted militia fought vicious skirmishes with British dragoons and captured straggling infantry as they

Morgan had hastily equipped some of his militia as dragoons. The Continental and militia dragoons charged into the British left flank and rear, as depicted by Steve Noon. (Gilbert and Gilbert)

Graham Turner '14

**THE CAPTURE OF TARLETON'S LIGHT ARTILLERY (PP. 74–75)**

The collapse of the green-clad Loyalist British Legion and the red-coated 7th Royal Fusiliers infantry exposed Tarleton's light artillery (**1**) to attack by Morgan's Continentals. The handful of blue-clad Royal Artillery gunners (**2**) fought valiantly for their guns, but they were quickly overwhelmed. In that era the loss of artillery was a terrible blow to prestige that not even Tarleton could conceal.

scoured the roads for the lucrative British baggage trains. The militia patrols seized loads of weaponry, and numerous horses and other property which they kept for themselves. Collins recalled: "Next day after receiving some small share of the plunder, and taking care to get as much powder as we could, we (the militia) were disbanded and retreated to our old haunts, where we obtained a few days rest." In his report to Greene, Morgan listed as army booty "one travelling forge, thirty-five baggage wagons, seventy negroes, and upwards of 100 dragoon horses, with all their musick. They destroyed most of the baggage which was immense."

Some of Morgan's militia remained to observe and report on Cornwallis' movements, but most left to protect their homes and families from Loyalist raiders.

The first body of British dragoons straggled into Cornwallis' camp that evening, "at which time his Lordship had the mortification to learn of the defeat of his detachment; the other, under Lieutenant Colonel Tarleton, appeared next morning." Cornwallis seems never to have been overly critical of his subordinates, but his tolerance of Tarleton's repeated calamities and excuses is baffling to a modern analyst. As was typical with the officer class of the era, Cornwallis placed the blame squarely upon the common soldiers, and penned a letter of exoneration to Tarleton: "You have forfeited no part of my esteem as an officer by the unfortunate event of the action of the 17th: The means you used to bring the enemy into action were able and masterly, and must ever do you honour. Your disposition was unexceptionable; the total misbehavior of the troops could alone have deprived you of the glory which was so justly your due."

MacKenzie's summary is more relevant. A short delay before the attack would have allowed the numerically superior British cavalry to assess Morgan's defense, the famished and exhausted infantry could have been given a brief rest, and the troops left behind with the baggage could have come forward. The artillery, to which the Americans had no counter, was not allowed to disrupt and demoralize the defenders. In typical fashion majors McArthur and Newmarsh, "officers who had held commissions long before our author [Tarleton] was born, and who had reputations to this day unimpeached," were not consulted. With a much longer delay Cornwallis could have drawn near, "the unattainment of which he has been so much and so unjustly censured" in Tarleton's memoir.

French military observer the Marquis de Chastellux praised Morgan's "modesty and simplicity" and expressed "astonishment" at the effect of the retrograde maneuver that resulted in the ultimate collapse of the British infantry. "But after the first discharge he made so dangerous a movement, that had he commanded the best disciplined troops in the world, I should be at a loss to account for it … it depended on General Morgan alone to have claimed the merit, and to have

Almost all "contemporary" art, like this 1820 example, depicted the romanticized clash between Washington and Tarleton after the battle had been decided. The clothing is wholly fictional. (Anne S. K. Brown Collection)

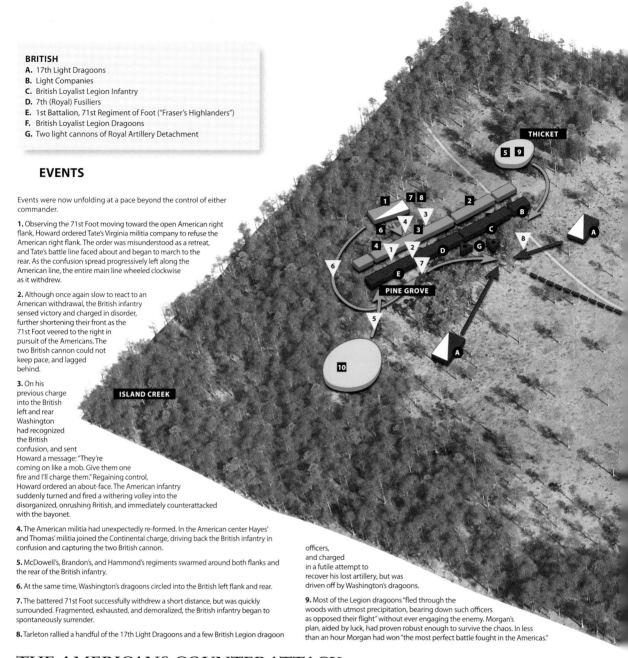

**BRITISH**
**A.** 17th Light Dragoons
**B.** Light Companies
**C.** British Loyalist Legion Infantry
**D.** 7th (Royal) Fusiliers
**E.** 1st Battalion, 71st Regiment of Foot ("Fraser's Highlanders")
**F.** British Loyalist Legion Dragoons
**G.** Two light cannons of Royal Artillery Detachment

## EVENTS

Events were now unfolding at a pace beyond the control of either commander.

**1.** Observing the 71st Foot moving toward the open American right flank, Howard ordered Tate's Virginia militia company to refuse the American right flank. The order was misunderstood as a retreat, and Tate's battle line faced about and began to march to the rear. As the confusion spread progressively left along the American line, the entire main line wheeled clockwise as it withdrew.

**2.** Although once again slow to react to an American withdrawal, the British infantry sensed victory and charged in disorder, further shortening their front as the 71st Foot veered to the right in pursuit of the Americans. The two British cannon could not keep pace, and lagged behind.

**3.** On his previous charge into the British left and rear Washington had recognized the British confusion, and sent Howard a message: "They're coming on like a mob. Give them one fire and I'll charge them." Regaining control, Howard ordered an about-face. The American infantry suddenly turned and fired a withering volley into the disorganized, onrushing British, and immediately counterattacked with the bayonet.

**4.** The American militia had unexpectedly re-formed. In the American center Hayes' and Thomas' militia joined the Continental charge, driving back the British infantry in confusion and capturing the two British cannon.

**5.** McDowell's, Brandon's, and Hammond's regiments swarmed around both flanks and the rear of the British infantry.

**6.** At the same time, Washington's dragoons circled into the British left flank and rear.

**7.** The battered 71st Foot successfully withdrew a short distance, but was quickly surrounded. Fragmented, exhausted, and demoralized, the British infantry began to spontaneously surrender.

**8.** Tarleton rallied a handful of the 17th Light Dragoons and a few British Legion dragoon officers, and charged in a futile attempt to recover his lost artillery, but was driven off by Washington's dragoons.

**9.** Most of the Legion dragoons "fled through the woods with utmost precipitation, bearing down such officers as opposed their flight" without ever engaging the enemy. Morgan's plan, aided by luck, had proven robust enough to survive the chaos. In less than an hour Morgan had won "the most perfect battle fought in the Americas."

# THE AMERICANS COUNTERATTACK, THE LEGION DRAGOONS FLEE

Events unfolded with startling rapidity. Howard ordered Tate's militia to refuse the right flank, but the order was misunderstood as a retreat. As confusion spread progressively left along the American line, the entire main line wheeled clockwise as it withdrew. Initially slow to react, the British infantry sensed victory and charged in disorder, further shortening their front. Howard ordered an about-face, the infantry fired a withering volley into the onrushing British, and counterattacked with the bayonet. The American militia had unexpectedly re-formed, and swarmed around both flanks of the British infantry while Washington's dragoons circled into the British rear. The battered 71st Foot withdrew to the first rise, but was quickly surrounded. The British infantry began to spontaneously surrender. Tarleton rallied a handful of dragoons and charged in a futile attempt to recover his lost artillery, but was driven off by Washington. Most of the Legion Dragoons fled without engaging the enemy, "bearing down such officers as opposed their flight."

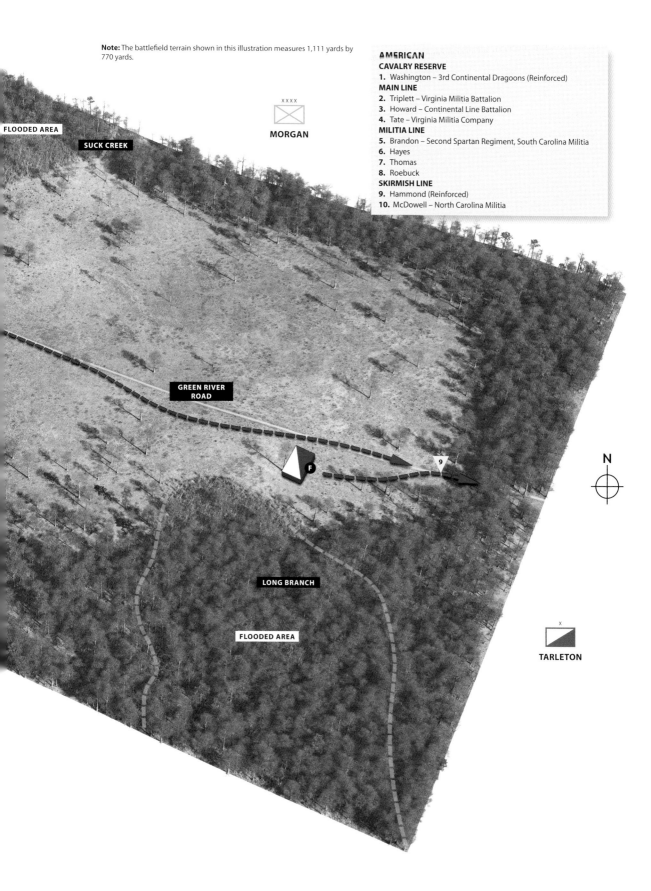

**Note:** The battlefield terrain shown in this illustration measures 1,111 yards by 770 yards.

FLOODED AREA

SUCK CREEK

xxxx
MORGAN

**AMERICAN**
**CAVALRY RESERVE**
1. Washington – 3rd Continental Dragoons (Reinforced)
**MAIN LINE**
2. Triplett – Virginia Militia Battalion
3. Howard – Continental Line Battalion
4. Tate – Virginia Militia Company
**MILITIA LINE**
5. Brandon – Second Spartan Regiment, South Carolina Militia
6. Hayes
7. Thomas
8. Roebuck
**SKIRMISH LINE**
9. Hammond (Reinforced)
10. McDowell – North Carolina Militia

GREEN RIVER
ROAD

F

9

N

LONG BRANCH

FLOODED AREA

x
TARLETON

Alonzo Chappel more correctly depicted the British and American dragoon uniforms. (Anne S. K. Brown Collection)

The most accurate depiction of the final dragoon clash appeared in Henry Cabot Lodge's *The Story of the Revolution*. (Lodge)

boasted of one of the boldest stratagems ever employed in the art of war. This is a merit however he never claimed." Morgan could in fact claim no merit for this maneuver; the credit for salvaging the situation belonged to Howard and his men. "Whatever was the motive of this singular manoeuvre, the result of it was the defeat of Tarleton, whose troops gave way without a possibility of rallying."

Even the jealous and irascible Sumter penned a brief letter (dated January 28, 1781) that concluded: "Upon which happy event I most heartily congratulate you."

Because of poor (or no) record keeping, accurate numbers of casualties in the southern battles are impossible to estimate. With no medical service, men like North Carolina militiaman William Meade who had his "rib broken by point of a bayonet, had his skull badly fractured by a Sword, and had a leg badly wounded by the stroke of a Cutlass," were cared for by comrades or local civilians as best they could.

British Army muster records, taken at irregular intervals, do not accurately reflect losses in this action. The important fact is that the heaviest losses were among the troops Cornwallis could least afford to lose, his invaluable Redcoats. Jeremiah Preston recalled: "it was stated we took 518 prisoners, but this was from report." The 1st Battalion of the 71st Foot was almost entirely captured or killed. "The Royal Fusiliers were, as a regiment, practically destroyed; their casualties amongst the men are not recorded, but they were very heavy. Of the nine officers present, Captain Helyar and Lieutenant Marshall were killed; Major Newmarsh and Lieutenants Harling and L'Estrange wounded. Their Colours, unfortunately, were, for the second time during this unhappy war, captured by the enemy. The affair at the Cowpens was the last in which the Fusiliers took part in the War of Independence; the few of them who escaped death or capture rejoined Lord Cornwallis's army, and were placed in garrison in South Carolina until that province was evacuated in 1782."

British historians accepted Tarleton's version of the battle, in which he had inflicted crippling losses upon the Americans, and this myth persisted well into the 20th century. Even today, Tarleton's so obviously self-serving and deceptive memoir is often cited as a definitive first-person account.

# EXPLOITING VICTORY: THE RACE TO THE DAN

The Americans had lopped off a quarter of Cornwallis' army, but Morgan's army remained in jeopardy. Cornwallis' major problem was the lack of adequate light infantry and the cavalry essential for reconnaissance: the 17th Light Dragoons (40 survivors) had been badly mauled, and the Legion dragoons (200 survivors) had proven completely useless against a determined foe. Still, he had the intact the 33rd Foot, the 23rd Foot (Royal Welch Fusiliers), the 2nd Battalion of the 71st Foot, Major-General Leslie's 1,400 or so fresh men (two battalions of the Foot Guards, and the von Bose Regiment with a detachment of jaegers), and about 250 Loyalist militia of dubious reliability. Cornwallis had good reason for optimism, since he outnumbered Greene two-to-one in line infantry.

Greene would need every bit of his organizational genius to maintain an army-in-being. He still hoped to mire Cornwallis in South Carolina. Fortune, in the form of Cornwallis' nagging concern for the safety of Ninety Six, favored the Americans. On the morning of January 19 Cornwallis moved slowly north from his camp on Turkey Creek, slogging along muddy paths toward Cherokee Ford and Tate's Ferry, the only crossings where his infantry and wagons could safely traverse the rain-swollen Broad River and turn back south to cut Morgan off from Ninety Six. Tarleton and the demoralized dragoons were sent west in a frantic search for Morgan.

Morgan, encumbered with prisoners, was thereby granted a head start. In the confused aftermath of the King's Mountain victory, the vast majority of Loyalist prisoners had escaped captivity, many to fight again, and Morgan was determined to move his prisoners beyond Cornwallis' reach. Early on the morning of January 18 he turned away from Ninety Six, and was already 20 miles (32km) north of Cowpens, near Gilbert Town. He would put as many river crossings as possible between him and Cornwallis, posting militia at every one to delay pursuit. On January 21 he sent the prisoners north under escort of Washington's dragoons to cross the Catawba, with orders to rejoin on the eastern shore near Sherrald's Ford.

Not until January 21 did Cornwallis discover that Tarleton was chasing a phantom, and recall him. In the pre-dawn hours of the next day the Legion dragoons, the Guards, and the 33rd Foot set off to the east.

On January 23 Morgan crossed the Catawba at Beattie's Ford. He briefly rested his troops, and burned all his extraneous baggage.

On the morning of January 24 Morgan sent the prisoners north toward the Salisbury depot, in North Carolina, under escort of Virginia and North Carolina militia whose enlistments had expired. Richard Swearingen said that "he was intrusted with a Part of the Prisoners they being sent off in Small Squads and Companies." Not all these militiamen departed. Jeremiah Preston said: "it was my choice to stay, for … [I] would have run away from my Father had I not been drafted."

Colonel Otho H. Williams and his Light Infantry were instrumental in distracting, harrying, and delaying Cornwallis' pursuit of Greene's army in the "Race to the Dan." (Lossing)

## Cornwallis' lost opportunity, January 18–25, 1781.

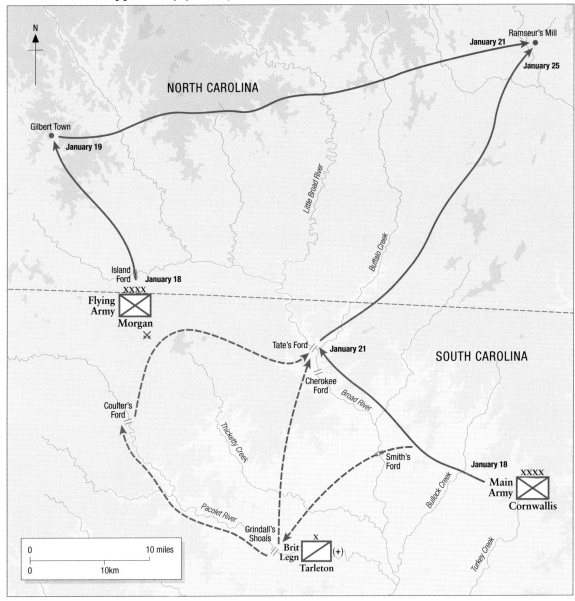

Most of the transport wagons followed the next day. By now Morgan suffered from sciatica that often kept him confined to bed in nearby houses, unable even to walk. In a dispatch to Greene he recommended Pickens as a successor.

The winter weather was atrocious, paralyzing both armies. Under drenching rain, the roads froze rock-hard at night thawing to deep glutinous mud in the day. Both armies were badly debilitated. Morgan took the time to post detachments at the river crossings, and set men to work to render fords impassable. Only Beattie's Ford was held open for refugees fleeing Loyalist raiders and British regulars who, despite explicit orders, were plundering the countryside. Resting his army at Ramseur's Mill, Cornwallis was feeling the

# The race to the Dan, January 21–February 15, 1781.

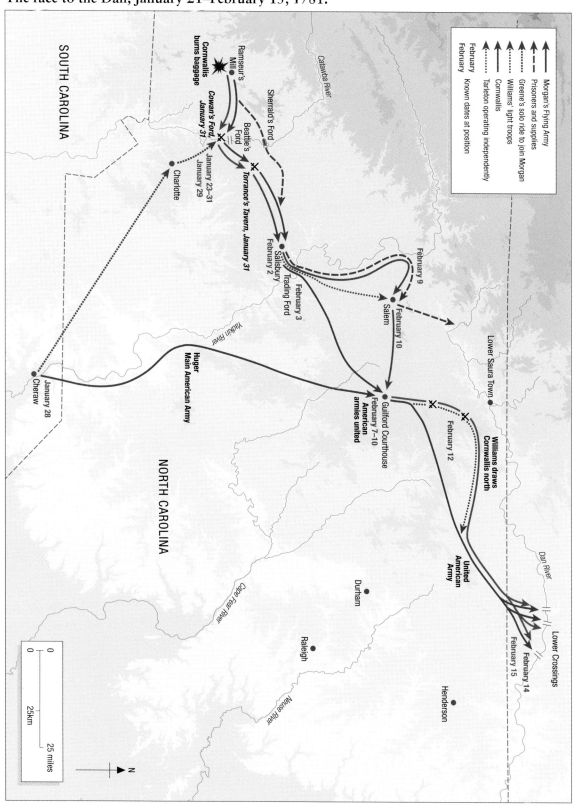

SOUTH CAROLINA

NORTH CAROLINA

Catawba River

Yadkin River

Cape Fear River

Neuse River

Dan River

Ramseur's Mill

Cornwallis burns baggage

Cowan's Ford, January 31

Sherrald's Ford

Beattie's Ford

January 23–31

January 29

Torrance's Tavern, January 31

Salisbury February 2

Trading Ford

February 3

February 9

Salem

February 10

Lower Saura Town

Charlotte

Huger Main American Army

Cheraw

January 28

Guilford Courthouse

February 7–10

American armies united

February 12

Williams draws Cornwallis north

United American Army

Lower Crossings

February 14

February 15

Durham

Raleigh

Henderson

**Legend:**
- Morgan's Flying Army
- Prisoners and supplies
- Greene's solo ride to join Morgan
- Williams' light troops
- Cornwallis
- Tarleton operating independently
- February — Known dates at position
- February

0 25km
0 25 miles

N

83

loss of his light troops, and realized that the only way to overtake Morgan was to make his entire army into light troops. He did the unthinkable. He ordered the destruction of all the usual comforts that slowed an army: the soldiers' tents and even the sacred rum supply; the officers' furniture, wine, crystal, and china were thrown into the bonfires. The general set the example by sacrificing his own baggage. Four wagons were kept as ambulances and to carry crucial supplies. Confiscated leather was hastily used to repair shoes.

On January 28 Greene finally abandoned his hope of drawing Cornwallis back south, and began a risky 100-mile ride through country infested with Loyalist militia to assume command of Morgan's Flying Army. He left orders for the rest of the army under General Isaac Huger to march to Salisbury. Meticulous as ever, he dispatched Lieutenant-Colonel Edward Carrington north to confiscate every available boat to facilitate crossing the broad Dan River in southern Virginia, should retreat be required.

On January 28 Cornwallis marched out to try to force a crossing of the Catawba, but heavy rain slowed his march, and by the afternoon of January 29 the river had overflowed its banks. On January 31 Greene and his party rode into the camp at Beattie's Ford and immediately convened an unusual council of war. From the log where they sat they could see a senior British officer, perhaps Cornwallis, evaluating the subsiding torrent.

Greene's main army would withdraw toward Salisbury, while about 800 local militiamen held two fords for as long as possible. The vulnerability was Cowan's Ford, four miles (6.5km) downstream from Beattie's, so Greene positioned 250 men there.

About dawn the next morning a diversionary cannonade at Beattie's Ford distracted the defenders. Cornwallis personally led the bulk of his infantry, muskets unloaded and bayonets fixed, into the frigid water at Cowan's Ford. The Loyalist guide somehow led the Redcoats into deeper water; Cowan's Ford split in mid-river into a deep "wagon ford" and a shallower "horse ford" that emerged about 1,250ft (380m) downstream. The noise of floundering men woke the sleeping American sentries. The militia rushed down to the banks, pouring a heavy fire into the Redcoats. According to a local Loyalist, "the river was full of 'em a snortin, a hollerin' and a drownin' until his Lordship reached the off bank." In hand-to-hand fighting the British forced the crossing. Cornwallis recorded four dead, but local Loyalists reported that "the river stunk with dead carcases" and counted British losses of at least a hundred.

Cornwallis' army surged toward Salisbury in driving rain and mud, slashing through clots of panicked refugees. That afternoon at Torrance's (sometimes called Tarrant's) Tavern, Tarleton's dragoons plowed murderously into about 50 disorganized militia and a milling mass of civilians. Tarleton reported another great victory, slaying "near 50 on the spot, wounded many in pursuit, and dispersed near 500." Another British officer "did not see ten dead bodies," and Tarleton suffered seven killed and an unknown number wounded.

On roads "up to our Knees in Mud it raining On us all the Way," Greene slogged slowly toward Trading Ford on the Yadkin River, destroying any local resources that might succor Cornwallis. On February 3 Greene achieved an extraordinarily hazardous crossing of the flooded Yadkin in boats. About dusk the British advance units clashed with a small militia rearguard that had orders to "give them a fire or Two and then Disperse down the River and

Cross in Canoes which they executed very well." The British could only stare glumly at the boats on the far bank. The next day Greene watched as Cornwallis arrived and in frustration shelled the far shore with artillery; Morgan and the Flying Army were already marching hard for Guilford Courthouse. Weather thwarted Huger's attempt to rendezvous at Salisbury, and Greene ordered him toward Guilford Courthouse.

Cornwallis dispatched Tarleton to locate another crossing of the Yadkin. He found Shallow Ford, 25 miles (40km) upstream, and on February 6 Cornwallis veered north.

In reaching Guilford Courthouse Huger had achieved an epic feat, marching his Continentals – many barefoot and nearly naked in the bitter weather – without a single straggler. On February 9 Greene convened another council. Greene feared the effect of continued flight on his troops' morale, but the recommendation of Huger, Otho Williams, and Morgan was unanimous. Greene was badly outnumbered, his men exhausted, and the North Carolina militia had largely failed to report. The retreat should continue. On February 10 Greene reluctantly placed Morgan on indefinite leave. He sent Morgan away in a more comfortable carriage, and later wrote that "Great generals are scarce – there are few Morgans to be found."

Cornwallis had pushed his army relentlessly, and was now at Salem, about 23 miles (37km) to the west. He believed he had Greene cornered; the lower Dan River fords were too deep to traverse in the rainy weather so Greene would now have to turn and move almost due north.

Greene's plan was to use Otho Williams' light infantry and Henry "Light Horse Harry" Lee's dragoons to screen the army and divert Cornwallis north while the main army headed east, 70 miles (110km) to the lower crossings. The effort commenced early on February 10. Cornwallis pursued, slowing his march to concentrate his forces, his rear harried by bands of American partisans. For two crucial days Williams and Lee skillfully held Cornwallis at arm's length in innumerable skirmishes, drawing him north, making him believe that they were screening the American army headed for the upper fords of the Dan near Lower Saura Town. The only notable incidents were when Cornwallis' men uncharacteristically surprised some of Williams' famished men at a luxurious bacon and cornmeal breakfast, and when Tarleton's men hacked apart a 14-year-old drummer caught by the roadside.

Not until February 12 did Cornwallis realize he had been tricked, when Williams broke contact and turned east for the final sprint. The next day, with Cornwallis at his heels, a despairing Williams thought he might have to confront Cornwallis to buy time, "to risque the Troops I have the Honor to Command and in doing that I risque everything." Nightly rest was now only two or three hours.

Early on February 14 a dispatch rider informed Williams that the army was safely across the Dan. He began a desperate 14-mile (22km) forced march, with Lee screening the rear. Late that night Lieutenant-Colonel Carrington was waiting with the boats. The men were ferried across, Lee's men swimming their horses alongside.

The next morning the British light troops arrived at the rain-swollen crossings of the biggest river in the region, to again see all the boats tied on the far shore. In 30 hours Cornwallis had driven his troops 40 miles (65km) over ghastly roads. Williams had covered the same distance in 20 hours.

# AFTERMATH

Cornwallis marched his battered army to the port at Wilmington, North Carolina, where he could be resupplied by sea. In the spring, Greene marched back into North Carolina and on March 15 confronted Cornwallis at Guilford Courthouse (see Angus Konstam's Campaign 109: *Guilford Courthouse 1781*). Cornwallis prevailed, but the leader of the opposition in Parliament acidly observed that "One more such victory would prove the ruin of the British army." Cornwallis abandoned the Carolinas and marched into Virginia to confront the elusive Lafayette, only to suffer encirclement and surrender at Yorktown (see Brendan Morrissey's Campaign 47: *Yorktown 1781*). Yorktown broke Parliament's will to continue the futile struggle in America, but it would take two long years to negotiate an end to the conflict.

Cornwallis eventually overcame the stigma of Yorktown. As Governor General of India he instituted a meritocracy in the colonial government and the East India Company, reformed courts, taxation, and education, and outlawed child slavery. He later became Master of Ordnance, then Lord Lieutenant and Commander-in-Chief of Ireland, where he defeated both Irish rebels and a French invasion. He was instrumental in passing the Act of Union that created the United Kingdom.

Somehow Cornwallis never lost faith in Tarleton, who responded by writing a memoir critical of his old commander. In it all things bad were attributed to others, all things glorious to Tarleton. Tarleton wrote that "[losses in] the action at the Cowpens, amounted to near three hundred on both sides, officers and men inclusive: This loss was almost equally shared; but the Americans took two pieces of cannon, the colours of the 7th Regiment, and near four hundred prisoners." He declared that "A diffuse comment upon this affair would be equally useless and tiresome," and then devoted five pages to describing Morgan's flawed deployment and to justification of his own actions. Subordinate officers penned rebuttals, but lacked the military rank, wealth, or royal connections of Tarleton. (Tarleton's mistress, the actress Mary Robinson, was the former mistress of young Prince of Wales and future King George IV.) Their work – with the exception of MacKenzie's *Strictures on Lt. Col. Tarleton's History*

Cornwallis regrouped at Wilmington, and then moved into Virginia in a fruitless effort to corner and destroy Lafayette's Continental army. Instead, he was trapped in Yorktown by French naval control of the Chesapeake Bay.

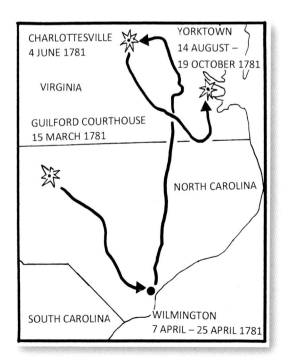

CHARLOTTESVILLE
4 JUNE 1781

YORKTOWN
14 AUGUST –
19 OCTOBER 1781

VIRGINIA

GUILFORD COURTHOUSE
15 MARCH 1781

NORTH CAROLINA

SOUTH CAROLINA

WILMINGTON
7 APRIL – 25 APRIL 1781

– is now little-known, Through royal connections Tarleton rose to the rank of general. In 1812 he was thwarted in his desire to command British forces in Spain when Wellington received the appointment, and he remained highly critical of the Iron Duke. He also served in Parliament, where he was a staunch protector of his family's slave-trading interests.

Humiliated by defeat and capture at Cowpens, Archibald McArthur complained that "the best troops in the service had been put under that boy [Tarleton] to be sacrificed." After being exchanged, in April 1781 McArthur was promoted to lieutenant-colonel of the 60th Foot (Royal Americans) and served with that regiment until Yorktown.

In this depiction by Jean-Matias Fontaine, Rochambeau and Washington jointly issue orders for the attack on Yorktown's defenses, October 14, 1781. (Anne S. K. Brown Collection)

Eventually promoted to brigadier, he served in Canada, the Caribbean, and Europe. He retired from the army in 1790, and died in Germany 15 years later.

Richard Hovenden, captured at Yorktown, was typical of many Loyalist officers. Exchanged the following December, he was taken into the British Army, but forever bore the stigma of a colonial. Frustrated by slow advancement he left the army and became a Justice of the Peace in Ireland. Other Loyalists, both officers and common soldiers, were relocated to Canadian land grants, Caribbean colonies, or quietly settled in as citizens of the new nation.

Nathanael Greene received generous grants of land and funds from the Carolinas and Georgia. He declined to serve as the new nation's Secretary of War, and died in 1786 aged 43.

Daniel Morgan suffered from sciatica, rheumatism, and severe hemorrhoids. In 1794 he was called back into service to suppress the Whiskey Rebellion in western Pennsylvania, and promoted to major-general.

Despite tactical victories, the rump British army left in South Carolina was penned into impotent coastal enclaves. The last British stronghold, Charlestown, was evacuated in December 1782. (Lodge)

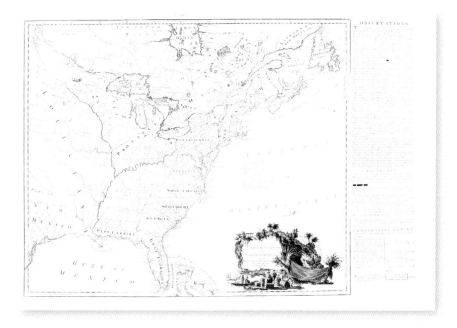

The 1783 Treaty of Paris ostensibly gave the new United States control of lands from the Appalachians to the Mississippi River, but continued British commercial influence in Florida (ceded to Spain) and the ill-defined border with Canada were significant factors leading to the War of 1812. (Library of Congress)

Although he had little appetite for politics, he served as a US Congressman, and died in 1802 on his 66th birthday.

Robert Kirkwood, captain of the Delaware Company, survived 32 Revolutionary War actions without a scratch. In 1791 he was killed fighting the Miami tribe in present-day Indiana, still a captain in the Regular Army.

Thomas Sumter recovered to command troops in the closing phases of the war. He served as a US Congressman and Senator. Fort Sumter in Charleston Harbor was named for him.

Wounded at Eutaw Springs (September 8, 1781), John Eager Howard served in the US Senate, and later became a leading philanthropist and prominent citizen of Baltimore.

Andrew Pickens was promoted to brigadier-general in the militia. Pickens became a wealthy planter, and in later years often served as a mediator between the Cherokee and the US government.

Thomas Brandon went on to become a brigadier-general of militia, member of the state legislature, and civil judge.

Of the 11 commemorative medals awarded for distinguished service in the Revolution, five were awarded for the Southern Campaign, and three for service at Cowpens. The inscription on Greene's gold medal translates "The Safety of the Southern Department" and "The Foe Conquered at Eutaw, 8th of September 1781," a battle Greene actually lost. (Lossing)

GOLD MEDAL AWARDED TO GREENE.[2]

# FINAL ANALYSIS

Morgan did not escape criticism for his brilliant victory. Tarleton's recitation of Morgan's flawed deployment can be readily dismissed, and armchair generals criticized Morgan. Historian J. B. O. Landrum wrote that Morgan was "severely censured for his choice of ground and for risking a battle under what appeared to be the most adverse of circumstances," with the Broad River behind "to cut off all retreat in the case of misfortune." But even that was part of Morgan's plan to make his militiamen "do or die."

The unique victory at the Cowpens was a confluence of many factors, among them Tarleton's ego, tactical recklessness, and his utter predictability. Another was the exhaustion of Tarleton's troops: he had ordered them to perform one too many superhuman feats. There is a military aphorism that no one can be brave every day, and Tarleton's troops were exhausted, physically and morally. "Some of the best troops in the service" just lay down in surrender.

Morgan's innate tactical genius allowed him to develop a plan that took maximum advantage of terrain, his own troops' strengths and weaknesses, and Tarleton's weaknesses. By taking the time to quiz his subordinates Morgan was able to develop an understanding of Tarleton. He formulated a subtle tactical trap, and "Bloody Ban" accommodated by rushing headlong into it. Most analysts have praised Morgan for the innovative defense in depth.

Morgan's leadership style was another key factor. Henry Wells of the Delaware Company said that, "The result of this victory is mainly due to the skill & bravery of Colonel Morgan & Washington for who could refuse to follow, & fight for such leaders."

Morgan took time to inspire the militia, and to painstakingly explain their role in his plan so that there would be no panic-stricken flight. Considerable credit must be given to the altogether unusual performance of

Morgan's medal reads "Victory, the Protector of Liberty" and "The Foe put to flight, taken or slain, at Cowpens, January 17th, 1781." (Lossing and NARA)

John Eager Howard's silver medal was inscribed: "Because, rushing suddenly on the wavering of the line of the foe, he gave a brilliant specimen of martial courage at the battle of Cowpens, January 17th, 1781." (Lossing)

William Washington's medal reads: "Because having vigorously pursued the foe with a small band of soldiers, he gave a brilliant specimen of innate valor in the battle of Cowpens, January 17th 1781." (Lossing)

the militia. Without their determination to stand, fight, and put an end to Bloody Ban the Continentals would have been left standing alone and surrounded. Without that determination Cowpens might well have been another Camden. Instead the militia, in part for personal reasons and in part because of Morgan's inspiration, stood its ground and inflicted unexpectedly high casualties on the British infantry.

The discipline and training of Howard's Continentals and Virginia militia were key factors. The militia would never have stood in the face of a British onslaught without the steadying effect of the line of Continental bayonets.

In the final analysis a great general needs both skill and luck, and both fell together for Daniel Morgan at Cowpens. There were several points at which Morgan's plan could have failed disastrously. The militia did, as Morgan undoubtedly feared, at first flee from Tarleton's dreaded cavalry. But then they rallied and spontaneously counterattacked. The misunderstood order that caused the main line of Continentals and highly disciplined militia to pivot backward inadvertently saved Morgan's right flank from being turned by Tarleton's best troops. Had Howard's order to refuse his right flank been correctly understood, the Continentals and Virginia militia would have remained exchanging volleys at point-blank range with Tarleton's best Redcoats, precisely the type of action that played to British strength. The 71st Foot would likely have overlapped the American right, with disastrous results. The unplanned withdrawal threw the British into even greater confusion; it was the unplanned consummation of Morgan's tactical trap.

History was made, and the fate of a nation decided.

## THE LEGACY OF COWPENS

The Cowpens battle was lauded by politicians and the public. Awards for military valor or achievement were unusual, and generally limited to Continentals. The most prestigious awards were one-of-a-kind medals awarded by Congress, designed for static display, not for wear with the uniform. Of the 11 such medals produced, three were for service at Cowpens: Daniel Morgan, John Eager Howard, and William Washington. Lesser awards included presentation swords or thoroughbred horses.

Today Cowpens is given limited (if any) space in most mainstream histories. In popular literature it is completely overshadowed by battles in

Cowpens lives on in the lineage of the US Navy. The World War II Light Aircraft Carrier USS *Cowpens* (CVL-25) and the modern Ticonderoga-class Guided Missile Cruiser USS *Cowpens* (CG-63) were named for the battle. (NARA, US Navy)

New England. The exception is the strange film *The Patriot*, which places a character based on Francis Marion in a prominent leadership role (facing both Cornwallis and arch-villain "Colonel Taverton") in a climactic battle clearly intended to represent Cowpens.

The battle is still studied by military officers as an example of a rare tactical double-envelopment, the "American Cannae" and the "most perfect battle fought in the Americas."

Cowpens lives on more visibly in the lineage of the US Navy. The light aircraft carrier USS *Cowpens* (CVL-25) served with distinction in the Central Pacific, Philippines, and off Okinawa from 1943 through 1945. The Ticonderoga-class guided-missile cruiser USS *Cowpens* (CG-63) launched the first Tomahawk missiles in the 2003 war with Iraq, and has served in humanitarian missions.

# THE BATTLEFIELD TODAY

Several important battlefields lie within a relatively small geographic area, and are well preserved. Major sites are marked on highway maps, and directions are marked by highway signage. Individual states have placed roadside historical markers locating smaller battle and skirmish sites. Markers in South Carolina are indexed by county at http://www.lat34north.com/HistoricMarkersSC/MarkerIndex.cfm; York, Cherokee, Spartanburg, and Union Counties are the most relevant.

Three recommended sites are the Cowpens, King's Mountain, and Blackstock's Farm sites. Cowpens and King's Mountain are preserved as National Military Parks, and Blackstock's is an undeveloped state site.

King's Mountain National Military Park preserves the entire battle site in rural York County, SC. The park includes interpretive displays, artifacts, weapons, and a clearly marked walking tour. The contiguous King's Mountain State Park has replicas of settlers' cabins, and a preserved massive two-story log structure typical of those built for defense against attacks by the Cherokee.

The entire Cowpens battle site is preserved as a national military park. The walking tour (dashed line) covers 1.3 miles (2.09km). (National Park Service)

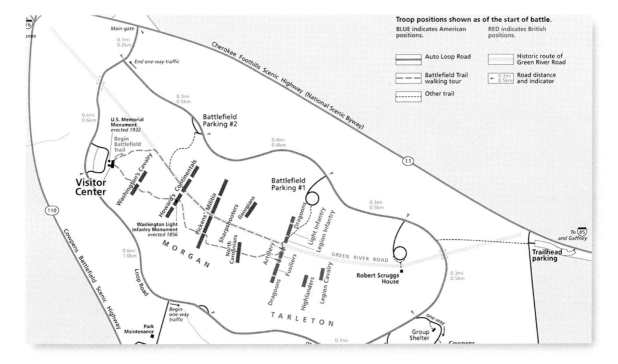

The Blackstock's battle site is mostly densely forested, but is of interest to those seeking a detailed understanding of the little-known but significant battle. The last segment of the unpaved access road follows the military crest of the ridge defended by Patriot militia, and a stone marker on a knoll is near the right end of the Patriot line. A sketch map is available at http://www.sctrails.net/trails/alltrails/palmetto%20trail/BlackstockPassage.html.

Detailed directions to the Cowpens National Battlefield Park, schedules of commemorative events, operating hours, and other useful information are available at http://www.nps.gov/cowp/index.htm. The visitor center includes interpretive displays and artifacts, and of particular interest is an accurate replica of a grasshopper gun. A loop walking trail identifies significant locations.

The site is subtly different from 1781. Period accounts describe low-lying swampy areas bounding the northeastern and southwestern edges of the battle space, and a distinctive rise to the west side of the Green River Road. Centuries of cattle grazing and erosion have subdued the already subtle topographic rises and washed sediment in to partially fill the old swampy areas. The net effect is that the "militia rise" that Morgan used to conceal his main line of Continentals has become even more subdued over the centuries.

The battlefield section of the park is maintained as a closely mown area with widely spaced trees, presenting long sight vistas. In 1781 the land was unimproved pasture, covered in waist-high native grasses interspersed with shrubs and trees. The best impression of what the battle site was actually like is provided by the areas of unimproved land that border the southwestern margin of the cleared area, easily accessible from the walking tour path.

One tactical factor that the park cannot guarantee is the low-lying ground fog described by some participants that further limited the range of vision on the cold, wet morning of the battle.

The Inn of the Patriots in Grover, North Carolina (theinnofthepatriots.com), provides a short guided tour of the inn's collection of artifacts, portraits of Patriot commanders by local artists, and reproduction small arms. (The facility houses the Presidential Culinary Museum for those less interested in the war.)

The Cherokee County History and Arts Museum in Gaffney, SC (http://www.cherokeecountyhistory.org/) includes displays of clothing and weapons. The York County Historical Museums system includes the Southern Revolutionary War Institute in York, SC (displays are limited) and restored buildings at Historic Brattonsville, the site of Huck's Defeat (July 12, 1780). Both are described at http://chmuseums.org/.

## Wargaming
Board simulations include *Battles of the American War of Independence: Volume 2 – Cowpens* (Markham Designs). Most gaming is done with miniatures, or as a scenario in the *British Grenadier!* system.

# FURTHER READING

Primary resources were the Federal Pension Applications preserved by the National Archives and Records Administration. Transcriptions by Will Graves of many pension applications relevant to the southern campaign are available at http://revwarapps.org/, but our transcriptions differ in detail as the result of varying interpretations of period handwriting. Sources listed below are chosen for their accessibility, including older resources readily purchasable as reprints or available online. Note that some online resources are transcriptions and may differ from the original. We have also utilized additional published and unpublished materials.

Babits, Lawrence E., *A Devil of a Whipping: The Battle of Cowpens*, University of North Carolina Press, Chapel Hill, 2001

Bearss, E. C., *Battle of Cowpens: A Documented Narrative and Troop Movement Maps*, Overmountain Press edition, Johnson City, TN, 1996

Bonk, David, *Continental vs Redcoat: American Revolutionary War*, Osprey Publishing, Oxford, UK, 2015

Buchanan, John, *The Road to Guilford Courthouse*, John Wiley and Sons, New York, 1997

Chartrand, Rene, *American Loyalist Troops 1775–84*, Osprey Publishing, Oxford, UK, 2008

Gilbert, Ed and Catherine Gilbert, *Patriot Militiaman in the American Revolution, 1775–82*, Osprey Publishing, Oxford, UK, 2015

Gilbert, Oscar and Catherine Gilbert, *True for the Cause of Liberty: The Second Spartan Regiment in the American Revolution*, Casemate, Havertown, PA and Oxford, UK, 2015

Groves, John Percy, Richard Cannon, and G. H. Waller, *Historical Records of the 7th or Royal Regiment of Fusiliers, Now Known as The Royal Fusiliers (The City of London Regiment), 1685–1903*, Frederick B. Guerin, London, UK, 1903

Johnson, William, *Sketches of the Life and Correspondence of Nathanael Greene*, Vol. II, A. E. Miller, Charleston, SC, 1822

Landrum, J. B. O., *Colonial and Revolutionary History of Upper South Carolina*, Shannon & Co., Greenville, SC, 1897

Lodge, H. C., *The Story of the Revolution*, Charles Scribner and Sons, New York, 1903

Lossing, B. J., *The Pictorial Field Book of The Revolution*, Vol. I, Harper Brothers, New York, 1850

MacKenzie, Roderick, *Strictures on Lt.Col. Tarleton's History of the Campaigns of 1780 and 1781, in the Southern Provinces of North America*, privately printed for the author, London, 1787

Moncure, John, *The Cowpens Staff Ride and Battlefield Tour*, Combat Studies Institute, U.S. Army Command and General Staff College, Fort Leavenworth, KS, 1996

Moss, B. G., *The Patriots at the Cowpens*, A Press, Greenville, SC, 1985

Myers, Theodorus B., *Cowpens Papers, Being Correspondence of Daniel Morgan and the Prominent Actors*, The News and Courier, Charleston, SC, 1881 (pamphlet reprint)

Ross, Charles (ed.), *Correspondence of Charles, First Marquis Cornwallis*, Vol. I, John Murray, London, UK, 1859

Stewart, David, *Sketches of the Character and Present State of the Highlanders of Scotland; With Details of the Military Service of the Highland Regiments*, Vol. II, Archibald Constable and Co., Edinburgh, UK; Longman, Hurst, Rees, Orme, Brown and Green, and Hurst, Robinson, and Co., London, UK, 1825

Tarleton, Banastre, *A History of the Campaigns of 1780 and 1781 in the Southern Provinces of North America*, T. Cadell, London, UK, 1787

# INDEX